Thomas Jefferson's
Life of Jesus

D1714484

TEMPLEGATE
Springfield, Ill.
62705

232.9
J

Thomas Jefferson was preoccupied for years with the project which resulted in this book. He wrote to his friend John Adams, "We must reduce our volume to the simple Evangelists; select, even from them, the very words only of Jesus . . . There will be found remaining the most sublime and benevolent code of morals which has ever been offered to man."

Although raised as an Anglican, Thomas Jefferson distrusted organized religion. "Laws provide against injury from others; but not from ourselves," he wrote. "God himself will not save men against their will. No man can conform his faith to the dictates of another. The life and essence of religion consists in the internal persuasion or belief of the mind . . . Compulsion in religion is distinguished peculiarly from compulsion in every other thing. I may grow rich by an art I am compelled to follow, I may recover health by medicines I am compelled to take . . . but I cannot be saved by a worship I disbelieve."

Jefferson, like many educated men of his era, was a deist. He believed that reason was a sufficient guide to truth, and did not believe in appeals to revelation. Reason, he felt, would reveal the existence of God and the need for moral harmony. It also led him to accept Jesus' teaching about an afterlife (since the doctrine could supplement and encourage the moral code Jesus recommended). "The doctrines of Jesus are simple," he wrote, "and tend all to the happiness of man. 1. That there is only one God, and he all perfect. 2. That there is a future state of rewards and punishments. 3. That to love God with all thy heart and thy neighbor as thyself, is the sum of religion."

The life of Jesus which Jefferson compiled from the scriptures reflects these opinions. His original effort was entitled, "The Philosophy of Jesus of Nazareth, extracted from the account of his life and doctrines, as given by Matthew, Mark, Luke and John; being an abridgement of the New Testament for the use of the Indians, unembarrassed with matters of fact or faith beyond the level of their comprehension." The last phrase, about the limitation of Indian comprehension, may have been deliberately witty. Jefferson himself was not a believer in those matters of faith which he found to be in conflict with reason. The Jesus who appears in this book is an ethical teacher, whose life ends with crucifixion. There is no resurrection here, nor are there miracles.

For Jefferson, religion and ethics were one and the same. "Say nothing of my religion," he wrote. "It is known to my God and myself alone. Its evidence before the world is to be sought in my life; if that has been honest and dutiful to society, the religion which has regulated it cannot be a bad one."

After his retirement from the Presidency Jefferson expanded the work he had done earlier. He arranged his selections from the gospels in parallel columns, including the Latin, Greek, and French texts along with the English. He made a note of the Roman law under which Jesus was tried by Pilate (it was his only written addition to the scriptures) and a concordance of the texts. His final version—known to many as "the Jefferson Bible"—was called "The Life and Morals of Jesus of Nazareth, as Extracted Textually from the Gospels." A copy of the book lies under the cornerstone of the Jefferson Memorial in Washington, placed there when the cornerstone was laid in 1939.

The religion of Jesus was important to Jefferson. "I am a Christian," he wrote to Dr. Benjamin Rush, "in the only sense in which he wished any one to be; sincerely attached to his doctrines, in preference to all others; ascribing to himself every human excellence, and believing he never claimed any other."

In many ways the religion of Thomas Jefferson must seem anachronistic today. The belief he held—that reason could show the existence of God and the afterlife—looks to modern rationalists like a piece of superstition. Most modern thinkers, religious and non-religious alike, find the faith in reason which animated Jefferson and his contemporaries naive and limited. The deism in which he believed has fallen out of fashion with almost everyone; at least it is no longer so optimistic.

We must, however, realize the sense of fresh life, of great and heroic experiment which lived in the hearts of Jefferson and other great minds of his age. They saw the world emerging into light after centuries of superstition, oppression and authoritarian government, established and corrupt religion. Now—with the power of reason given at birth to all men—man could begin to free himself and create for himself a place on earth worthy of his nature. The model of government proposed by Jefferson was based in the same faith which inspired his confident interpretation of Christianity: a nation of educated, land-holding, largely self-sufficient farmers, held together by as few enforced agreements as possible. But this nation could exist only where some ethical standards, some binding truths about human beings, their conduct, their destiny, were held as "self-evident."

The fashion today is to deny that any truths are self-evident. Perhaps the cynicism is justified. But the vision of people like Jefferson appeals to something strong in us. There is still an excitement in his vow of "eternal hostility against every form of tyranny over the mind of man." Religion, in Jefferson's view of things, was central to this battle and to this liberation. Where religion itself grew fat, established, and complacent in its mission it betrayed the best aspect of its unique vocation. There is something to be learned over again (or learned, maybe, for the first time) by reading this selection of Jesus' words. Whether or not we agree with Jefferson's perhaps too easy dismissal of everything which scandalized him in the gospels, it is important and helpful to see Christ's words presented as clearly as they are here, challenging us to see them as the liberating words they are.

Jefferson, early in his career, worked to disestablish the church in Virginia. There could be no true religious liberty or real tolerance, he believed, where the church and state lived in official wedlock. His opposition to the establishment of religion (an opposition carried on for the sake of *pure* religion, Jefferson believed) was misunderstood by many church people, and Jefferson resented it. He regarded his arrangement of scripture as "a document in proof that *I* am a *real* Christian, that is to say, a disciple of the doctrines of Jesus."

Religion and religious liberty were so much at the heart of Jefferson's concern as a citizen that they edge out his presidency in the epitaph he composed for himself: "Here was buried Thomas Jefferson, author of the Declaration of American Independence, of the statute of Virginia for religious freedom, and father of the University of Virginia."

Louis Michaels

On the following pages are facsimiles of Jefferson's handwritten title page and table of texts.

The

Life and Morals

of

Jesus of Nazareth

Extracted textually

from the Gospels

in

Greek, Latin

French & English.

M. 26. 14—16. Judas undertakes to point out Jesus.

17—20. L. 22. 24—27 J. 13. 2. 4—17 21—26. 31. 34. 35. M. 26. 31. 33.

L. 22. 33—34. M. 26. 35—45. precepts to his disciples, *washes their feet* trou-ble of mind and prayer.

J. 18 1—3. M. 26. 48—50. Judas conducts the officers to Jesus.

J. 18. 4—8. M. 26. 50—52. 55. 56. Mk. 14. 51. 52. M. 26. 57. J. 18. 15. 16. 18. 17

J. 18 25. 26. 27. M. 26. 75. J. 18. 19—23. Mk. 14. 55—61.

L. 22. 67. 68. 70. Mk. 14. 63—65. he is arrested & carried before Caiaphas the High priest & is condemned.

J. 18. 28—31. 33—38. L. 23. 5. M. 27. 13. is then carried to Pilate.

L. 23. 6—12. who sends him to Herod.

L. 23. 13—16. M. 27. 15—23. 26. recieves him back, scourges and delivers him to execution.

M. 27. 27. 29—31. 3—8. L. 23. 26—32. J. 19. 17—24. M. 27. 39—43.

L. 23 39—41. 34. J. 19. 25—27. M. 27. 46—55. 56. his crucifixion. death and burial.

J. 19. 31—34. 38—42. M. 27. 60. his burial.

THE LIFE AND MORALS

OF

JESUS OF NAZARETH.

I.

Joseph and Mary go to Bethlehem, Where Jesus is Born.

AND it came to pass in those days, that there went out a decree from Caesar Augustus, that all the world should be taxed.

2 *(And* this taxing was first made when Cyrenius was governor of Syria.)

3 And all went to be taxed, every one into his own city.

4 And Joseph also went up from Galilee, out of the city of Nazareth, into Judaea, unto the city of

David, which is called Bethlehem, (because he was of the house and lineage of David,)

5 To be taxed with Mary his espoused wife, being great with child.

6 And so it was, that, while they were there, the days were accomplished that she should be delivered.

7 And she brought forth her firstborn son, and wrapped him in swaddling clothes, and laid him in a manger; because there was no room for them in the inn.

II.

He is Circumcised and Named and they Return to Nazareth.

AND when eight days were accomplished for the circumcising of the child, his name was called JESUS.

2 And when they had performed all things according to the law of the Lord, they returned into Galilee, to their own city Nazareth.

III.

At Twelve Years of Age He Accompanies his Parents to Jerusalem and Returns.

AND the child grew, and waxed strong in spirit, filled with wisdom: and the grace of God was upon him.

2 And when he was twelve years old, they went up to Jerusalem after the custom of the feast.

3 And when they had fulfilled the days, as they returned, the child Jesus tarried behind in Jerusalem; and Joseph and his mother knew not *of it.*

4 But they, supposing him to have been in the company, went a day's journey; and they sought him among *their* kinsfolk and acquaintance.

5 And when they found him not, they turned back again to Jerusalem, seeking him.

6 And it came to pass, that after three days they found him in the temple, sitting in the midst of the doctors, both hearing them, and asking them questions.

7   And all that heard him were astonished at his understanding and answers.

8   And when they saw him, they were amazed: and his mother said unto him, Son, why hast thou thus dealt with us? behold, thy father and I have sought thee sorrowing.

9   And he went down with them, and came to Nazareth, and was subject unto them: but his mother kept all these sayings in her heart.

10   And Jesus increased in wisdom and stature, and in favour with God and man.

IV.

John Baptizes in Jordan.

NOW in the fifteenth year of the reign of Tibe· rıus Caesar, Pontius Pilate being governor of Judaea, and Herod being tetrarch of Galilee, and his brother Philip tetrarch of Ituraea and of the region of Trachonitis, and Lysanias the tetrarch of Abilene,

2 Annas and Caiaphas being the high priests, the word of God came unto John the son of Zacharias in the wilderness.

3 John did baptize in the wilderness, and preach the baptism of repentance for the remission of sins.

4 And the same John had his raiment of camel's hair, and a leathern girdle about his loins; and his meat was locusts and wild honey.

5 ¶ Then went out to him Jerusalem, and all Judaea, and all the region round about Jordan;

6 And were baptized of him in Jordan, confessing their sins.

V.

Jesus is Baptized at 30 Years of Age.

THEN cometh Jesus from Galilee to Jordan unto John, to be baptized of him.

2 And Jesus himself began to be about thirty years of age, being (as was supposed) the son of Joseph, which was *the son* of Heli.

VI.

Drives the Traders Out of the Temple.

AFTER this he went down to Capernaum, he, and his mother, and his brethren, and his disciples: and they continued there not many days.

2 ¶ And the Jews' passover was at hand, and Jesus went up to Jerusalem;

3 And found in the temple those that sold oxen and sheep and doves, and the changers of money sitting:

4 And when he had made a scourge of small cords, he drove them all out of the temple, and the sheep, and the oxen; and poured out the changers' money, and overthrew the tables;

5 And said unto them that sold doves, Take these things hence; make not my Father's house an house of merchandise.

VII.

He Baptizes, but Retires into Galilee on the Death of John.

AFTER these things came Jesus and his disciples into the land of Judaea; and there he tarried with them, and baptized.

2 ¶ Now when Jesus had heard that John was cast into prison, he departed into Galilee;

3 For Herod himself had sent forth and laid hold upon John, and bound him in prison for Herodias' sake, his brother Philip's wife: for he had married her.

4 For John had said unto Herod, It is not lawful for thee to have thy brother's wife.

5 Therefore Herodias had a quarrel against him, and would have killed him; but she could not:

6 For Herod feared John, knowing that he was a just man and an holy, and observed him; and when he heard him, he did many things, and heard him gladly.

7 And when a convenient day was come, that Herod on his birthday made a supper to his lords, high captains, and chief *estates* of Galilee;

8 And when the daughter of the said Herodias came in, and danced, and pleased Herod and them that sat with him, the king said unto the damsel, Ask of me whatsoever thou wilt, and I will give *it* thee.

9 And he sware unto her, Whatsoever thou shalt ask of me, I will give *it* thee, unto the half of my kingdom.

10 And she went forth, and said unto her mother, What shall I ask? And she said, The head of John the Baptist.

11 And she came in straightway with haste unto the king, and asked, saying, I will that thou give me by and by in a charger the head of John the Baptist.

12 And the king was exceeding sorry; *yet* for his oath's sake, and for their sakes which sat with him, he would not reject her.

13 And immediately the king sent an executioner, and commanded his head to be brought: and he went and beheaded him in the prison,

14 And brought his head in a charger, and gave it to the damsel: and the damsel gave it to her mother.

VIII.

He Teaches in the Synagogue.

AND they went into Capernaum; and straightway on the sabbath day he entered into the
synagogue, and taught.

2 And they were astonished at his doctrine:
for he taught them as one that had authority, and
not as the scribes.

IX.

Explains the Sabbath.

AT that time Jesus went on the sabbath day
through the corn; and his disciples were an
hungred, and began to pluck the ears of corn, and
to eat.

2 But when the Pharisees saw *it*, they said
unto him, Behold, thy disciples do that which is
not lawful to do upon the sabbath day.

3 But he said unto them, Have ye not read
what David did, when he was an hungred, and
they that were with him;

4 How he entered into the house of God, and did eat the shew-bread, which was not lawful for him to eat, neither for them which were with him, but only for the priests?

5 Or have ye not read in the law, how that on the sabbath days the priests in the temple profane the sabbath, and are blameless?

6 ¶ And when he was departed thence, he went into their synagogue:

7 And, behold, there was a man which had *his* hand withered. And they asked him, saying, Is it lawful to heal on the sabbath days? that they might accuse him.

8 And he said unto them, What man shall there be among you, that shall have one sheep, and if it fall into a pit on the sabbath day, will he not lay hold on it, and lift *it* out?

9 How much then is a man better than a sheep? Wherefore it is lawful to do well on the sabbath days.

10 And he said unto them, The sabbath was made for man, and not man for the sabbath.

11 ¶ Then the Pharisees went out, and held a council against him, how they might destroy him.

12   But when Jesus knew *it*, he withdrew himself from thence: and great multitudes followed him, and he healed them all.

X.

Call of His Disciples.

AND it came to pass in those days, that he went out into a mountain to pray, and continued all night in prayer to God.

2   And when it was day, he called *unto him* his disciples: and of them he chose twelve, whom also he named apostles;

3   Simon, (whom he also named Peter,) and Andrew his brother, James and John, Philip and Bartholomew,

4   Matthew and Thomas, James the *son* of Alphaeus, and Simon called Zelotes,

5   And Judas *the brother* of James, and Judas Iscariot, which also was the traitor.

6   And he came down with them, and stood in the plain, and the company of his disciples, and a great multitude of people out of all Judaea and

Jerusalem, and from the sea coast of Tyre and Sidon, which came to hear him, and to be healed of their diseases.

XI.

The Sermon on the Mount.

AND seeing the multitudes, he went up into a mountain: and when he was set, his disciples came unto him:

2 And he opened his mouth, and taught them, saying,

3 Blessed *are* the poor in spirit: for theirs is the kingdom of heaven.

4 Blessed *are* they that mourn: for they shall be comforted.

5 Blessed *are* the meek: for they shall inherit the earth.

6 Blessed *are* they which do hunger and thirst after righteousness: for they shall be filled.

7 Blessed *are* the merciful: for they shall obtain mercy.

8 Blessed *are* the pure in heart: for they shall see God.

9 Blessed *are* the peacemakers; for they shall be called the children of God.

10 Blessed *are* they which are persecuted for righteousness' sake: for theirs is the kingdom of heaven.

11 Blessed are ye, when *men* shall revile you, and persecute *you*, and shall say all manner of evil against you falsely, for my sake.

12 Rejoice, and be exceeding glad: for great *is* your reward in heaven: for so persecuted they the prophets which were before you.

13 But woe unto you that are rich! for ye have received your consolation.

14 Woe unto you that are full! for ye shall hunger. Woe unto you that laugh now! for ye shall mourn and weep.

15 Woe unto you, when all men shall speak well of you! for so did their fathers to the false prophets.

16 ¶ Ye are the salt of the earth: but if the salt have lost his savour, wherewith shall it be salted?

it is thenceforth good for nothing, but to be cast out, and to be trodden under foot of men.

17 Ye are the light of the world. A city that is set on an hill cannot be hid.

18 Neither do men light a candle, and put it under a bushel, but on a candlestick; and it giveth light unto all that are in the house.

19 Let your light so shine before men, that they may see your good works, and glorify your Father which is in heaven.

20 ¶ Think not that I am come to destroy the law, or the prophets: I am not come to destroy, but to fulfil.

21 For verily I say unto you, Till heaven and earth pass, one jot or one tittle shall in no wise pass from the law, till all be fulfilled.

22 Whosoever therefore shall break one of these least commandments, and shall teach men so, he shall be called the least in the kingdom of heaven: but whosoever shall do and teach *them,* the same shall be called great in the kingdom of heaven.

23 For I say unto you, That except your righteousness shall exceed *the righteousness* of the

scribes and Pharisees, ye shall in no case enter into the kingdom of heaven.

24 ¶ Ye have heard that it was said by them of old time, Thou shalt not kill; and whosoever shall kill shall be in danger of the judgment:

25 But I say unto you, That whosoever is angry with his brother without a cause shall be in danger of the judgment: and whosoever shall say to his brother, Raca, shall be in danger of the council; but whosoever shall say, Thou fool, shall be in danger of hell fire.

26 Therefore if thou bring thy gift to the altar, and there rememberest that thy brother hath ought against thee;

27 Leave there thy gift before the altar, and go thy way; first be reconciled to thy brother, and then come and offer thy gift.

28 Agree with thine adversary quickly, whiles thou art in the way with him; lest at any time the adversary deliver thee to the judge, and the judge deliver thee to the officer, and thou be cast into prison.

3

29 Verily I say unto thee, Thou shalt by no means come out thence, till thou hast paid the uttermost farthing.

30 ¶ Ye have heard that it was said by them of old time, Thou shalt not commit adultery:

31 But I say unto you, That whosoever looketh on a woman to lust after her hath committed adultery with her already in his heart.

32 And if thy right eye offend thee, pluck it out, and cast *it* from thee: for it is profitable for thee that one of thy members should perish, and not *that* thy whole body should be cast into hell.

33 And if thy right hand offend thee, cut it off, and cast *it* from thee: for it is profitable for thee that one of thy members should perish, and not *that* thy whole body should be cast into hell.

34 ¶ It hath been said, Whosoever shall put away his wife, let him give her a writing of divorcement:

35 But I say unto you, That whosoever shall put away his wife, saving for the cause of fornication, causeth her to commit adultery: and whosoever shall marry her that is divorced committeth adultery.

36 ¶ Again, ye have heard that it hath been said by them of old time, Thou shalt not forswear thyself, but shalt perform unto the Lord thine oaths:

37 But I say unto you, Swear not at all; neither by heaven; for it is God's throne:

38 Nor by the earth; for it is his footstool: neither by Jerusalem; for it is the city of the great King.

39 Neither shalt thou swear by thy head, because thou canst not make one hair white or black.

40 But let your communication be, Yea, yea; Nay, nay: for whatsoever is more than these cometh of evil.

41 ¶ Ye have heard that it hath been said, An eye for an eye, and a tooth for a tooth:

42 But I say unto you, That ye resist not evil: but whosoever shall smite thee on thy right cheek, turn to him the other also.

43 And if any man will sue thee at the law, and take away thy coat, let him have *thy* cloak also.

44 And whosoever shall compel thee to go a mile, go with him twain.

45   Give to him that asketh thee, and from him that would borrow of thee turn not thou away.

46   ¶ Ye have heard that it hath been said, Thou shalt love thy neighbour, and hate thine enemy.

47   But I say unto you, Love your enemies, bless them that curse you, do good to them that hate you, and pray for them which despitefully use you, and persecute you;

48   That ye may be the children of your Father which is in heaven: for he maketh his sun to rise on the evil and on the good, and sendeth rain on the just and on the unjust.

49   For if ye love them which love you, what reward have ye? do not even the publicans the same?

50   And if ye salute your brethren only, what do ye more *than others?* do not even the publicans so?

51   And if ye lend to *them* of whom ye hope to receive, what thank have ye? for sinners also lend to sinners, to receive as much again.

52   But love ye your enemies, and do good, and lend, hoping for nothing again; and your reward shall be great, and ye shall be the children of the Highest: for he is kind unto the unthankful and *to* the evil.

53   Be ye therefore merciful, as your Father also is merciful.

54   Take heed that ye do not your alms before men, to be seen of them: otherwise ye have no reward of your Father which is in heaven.

55   Therefore when thou doest *thine* alms, do not sound a trumpet before thee, as the hypocrites do in the synagogues and in the streets, that they may have glory of men.   Verily I say unto you, They have their reward.

56   But when thou doest alms, let not thy left hand know what thy right hand doeth:

57   That thine alms may be in secret: and thy Father which seeth in secret himself shall reward thee openly.

58   ¶ And when thou prayest, thou shalt not be as the hypocrites *are:* for they love to pray standing in the synagogues and in the corners of the streets, that they may be seen of men.   Verily I say unto you, They have their reward.

59   But thou, when thou prayest, enter into thy closet, and when thou hast shut thy door, pray to thy Father which is in secret; and thy Father which seeth in secret shall reward thee openly.

60　But when ye pray, use not vain repetitions, as the heathen *do:* for they think that they shall be heard for their much speaking.

61　Be not ye therefore like unto them: for your Father knoweth what things ye have need of, before ye ask him.

62　After this manner therefore pray ye: Our Father which art in heaven, Hallowed be thy name.

63　Thy kingdom come. Thy will be done in earth, as *it is* in heaven.

64　Give us this day our daily bread.

65　And forgive us our debts, as we forgive our debtors.

66　And lead us not into temptation, but deliver us from evil: For thine is the kingdom, and the power, and the glory, for ever. Amen.

67　For if ye forgive men their trespasses, your heavenly Father will also forgive you:

68　But if ye forgive not men their trespasses, neither will your Father forgive your trespasses.

69　¶ Moreover when ye fast, be not, as the hypocrites, of a sad countenance: for they disfigure their faces, that they may appear unto men to fast. Verily I say unto you, They have their reward.

70 But thou, when thou fastest, anoint thine head, and wash thy face;

71 That thou appear not unto men to fast, but unto thy Father which is in secret: and thy Father, which seeth in secret, shall reward thee openly.

72 ¶ Lay not up for yourselves treasures upon earth, where moth and rust doth corrupt, and where thieves break through and steal:

73 But lay up for yourselves treasures in heaven, where neither moth nor rust doth corrupt, and where thieves do not break through nor steal.

74 For where your treasure is, there will your heart be also.

75 The light of the body is the eye: if therefore thine eye be single, thy whole body shall be full of light.

76 But if thine eye be evil, thy whole body shall be full of darkness. If therefore the light that is in thee be darkness, how great *is* that darkness!

77 No man can serve two masters: for either he will hate the one, and love the other; or else he will hold to the one, and despise the other. Ye cannot serve God and mammon,

78   Therefore I say unto you, Take no thought for your life, what ye shall eat, or what ye shall drink; nor yet for your body, what ye shall put on. Is not the life more than meat, and the body than raiment?

79   Behold the fowls of the air: for they sow not, neither do they reap, nor gather into barns; yet your heavenly Father feedeth them.   Are ye not much better than they?

80   Which of you by taking thought can add one cubit unto his stature?

81   And why take ye thought for raiment?   Consider the lilies of the field, how they grow; they toil not, neither do they spin:

82   And yet I say unto you, That even Solomon in all his glory was not arrayed like one of these.

83   Wherefore, if God so clothe the grass of the field, which today is, and tomorrow is cast into the oven, *shall he* not much more *clothe* you, O ye of little faith?

84   Therefore take no thought, saying, What shall we eat? or, What shall we drink? or, Wherewithal shall we be clothed?

85 (For after all these things do the Gentiles seek:) for your heavenly Father knoweth that ye have need of all these things.

86 But seek ye first the kingdom of God, and his righteousness; and all these things shall be added unto you.

87 Take therefore no thought for the morrow: for the morrow shall take thought for the things of itself. Sufficient unto the day *is* the evil thereof.

88 Judge not, that ye be not judged.

89 For with what judgment ye judge, ye shall be judged: and with what measure ye mete, it shall be measured to you again.

90 Give, and it shall be given unto you; good measure, pressed down, and shaken together, and running over, shall men give into your bosom. For with the same measure that ye mete withal it shall be measured to you again.

91 And why beholdest thou the mote that is in thy brother's eye, but considerest not the beam that is in thine own eye?

92 Or how wilt thou say to thy brother, Let me pull out the mote out of thine eye; and, behold, a beam *is* in thine own eye?

93   Thou hypocrite, first cast out the beam out of thine own eye; and then shalt thou see clearly to cast out the mote out of thy brother's eye.

94   ¶ Give not that which is holy unto the dogs, neither cast ye your pearls before swine, lest they trample them under their feet, and turn again and rend you.

95   ¶ Ask, and it shall be given you; seek, and ye shall find; knock, and it shall be opened unto you:

96   For every one that asketh receiveth; and he that seeketh findeth; and to him that knocketh it shall be opened.

97   Or what man is there of you, whom if his son ask bread, will he give him a stone?

98   Or if he ask a fish, will he give him a serpent?

99   If ye then, being evil, know how to give good gifts unto your children, how much more shall your Father which is in heaven give good things to them that ask him?

100   Therefore all things whatsoever ye would that men should do to you, do ye even so to them: for this is the law and the prophets,

101 ¶ Enter ye in at the strait gate; for wide *is* the gate, and broad *is* the way, that leadeth to destruction, and many there be which go in thereat:

102 Because strait *is* the gate, and narrow *is* the way, which leadeth unto life, and few there be that find it.

103 ¶ Beware of false prophets, which come to you in sheep's clothing, but inwardly they are ravening wolves.

104 Ye shall know them by their fruits. Do men gather grapes of thorns, or figs of thistles?

105 Even so every good tree bringeth forth good fruit; but a corrupt tree bringeth forth evil fruit.

106 A good tree cannot bring forth evil fruit, neither *can* a corrupt tree bring forth good fruit.

107 Every tree that bringeth not forth good fruit is hewn down, and cast into the fire.

108 Wherefore by their fruits ye shall know them.

109 A good man out of the good treasure of the heart bringeth forth good things: and an evil man out of the evil treasure bringeth forth evil things.

110 But I say unto you, That every idle word that men shall speak, they shall give account thereof in the day of judgment.

111 For by thy words thou shalt be justified, and by thy words thou shalt be condemned.

112 ¶ Therefore whosoever heareth these sayings of mine, and doeth them, I will liken him unto a wise man, which built his house upon a rock:

113 And the rain descended, and the floods came, and the winds blew, and beat upon that house; and it fell not: for it was founded upon a rock.

114 And every one that heareth these sayings of mine, and doeth them not, shall be likened unto a foolish man, which built his house upon the sand:

115 And the rain descended, and the floods came, and the winds blew and beat upon that house; and it fell: and great was the fall of it.

116 ¶ And it came to pass, when Jesus had ended these sayings, the people were astonished at his doctrine:

117 For he taught them as *one* having authority, and not as the scribes.

XII.

Exhorts.

WHEN he was come down from the mountain, great multitudes followed him.

2 And he marvelled because of their unbelief. And he went round about the villages, teaching.

3 ¶ Come unto me, all *ye* that labour and are heavy laden, and I will give you rest.

4 Take my yoke upon you, and learn of me; for I am meek and lowly in heart: and ye shall find rest unto your souls.

5 For my yoke *is* easy, and my burden is light.

XIII.

A Woman Annointeth Him.

AND one of the Pharisees desired him that he would eat with him. And he went into the Pharisee's house, and sat down to meat.

2 And, behold, a woman in the city, which was a sinner, when she knew that *Jesus* sat at meat in

the Pharisee's house, brought an alabaster box of ointment,

3 And stood at his feet behind *him* weeping, and began to wash his feet with tears, and did wipe *them* with the hairs of her head, and kissed his feet, and anointed *them* with the ointment.

4 Now when the Pharisee which had bidden him saw *it*, he spake within himself, saying, This man, if he were a prophet, would have known who and what manner of woman *this is* that toucheth him: for she is a sinner.

5 And Jesus answering said unto him, Simon, I have somewhat to say unto thee. And he saith, Master, say on.

6 There was a certain creditor which had two debtors: the one owed five hundred pence, and the other fifty.

7 And when they had nothing to pay, he frankly forgave them both. Tell me therefore, which of them will love him most?

8 Simon answerd and said, I suppose that *he* to whom he forgave most. And he said unto him, Thou hast rightly judged.

9 And he turned to the woman, and said unto Simon, Seest thou this woman? I entered into thine house, thou gavest me no water for my feet: but she hath washed my feet with tears, and wiped *them* with the hairs of her head.

10 Thou gavest me no kiss: but this woman since the time I came in hath not ceased to kiss my feet.

11 My head with oil thou didst not anoint: but this woman hath anointed my feet with ointment.

12 Wherefore I say unto thee, Her sins, which are many, are forgiven; for she loved much: but to whom little is forgiven, *the same* loveth little.

13 And he said unto her, Thy sins are forgiven.

14 And they that sat at meat with him began to say within themselves, Who is this that forgiveth sins also?

15 And he said to the woman, Thy faith hath saved thee; go in peace.

XIV

Precepts.

THERE came then his brethren and his mother, and, standing without, sent unto him, calling him.

2   And the multitude sat about him, and they said unto him, Behold, thy mother and thy brethren without seek for thee.

3   And he answered them, saying, Who is my mother, or my brethren?

4   And he looked round about on them which sat about him, and said, Behold my mother and my brethren!

5   For whosoever shall do the will of God, the same is my brother, and my sister, and mother.

6   In the mean time, when there were gathered together an innumerable multitude of people, insomuch that they trode one upon another, he began to say unto his disciples first of all, Beware ye of the leaven of the Pharisees, which is hypocrisy.

7 For there is nothing covered, that shall not be revealed; neither hid, that shall not be known.

8 Therefore whatsoever ye have spoken in darkness shall be heard in the light; and that which ye have spoken in the ear in closets shall be proclaimed upon the housetops.

9 And I say unto you my friends, Be not afraid of them that kill the body, and after that have no more that they can do.

10 But I will forewarn you whom ye shall fear: Fear him, which after he hath killed hath power to cast into hell; yea, I say unto you, Fear him.

11 Are not five sparrows sold for two farthings, and not one of them is forgotten before God?

12 But even the very hairs of your head are all numbered. Fear not therefore; ye are of more value than many sparrows.

13 ¶ And one of the company said unto him, Master, speak to my brother, that he divide the inheritance with me.

14 And he said unto him, Man, who made me a judge or a divider over you?

15 And he said unto them, Take heed, and beware of covetousness: for a man's life consisteth

4

not in the abundance of the things which he possesseth.

XV.

Parable of the Rich Man.

AND he spake a parable unto them, saying, The ground of a certain rich man brought forth plentifully:

2 And he thought within himself, saying, What shall I do, because I have no room where to bestow my fruits?

3 And he said, This will I do: I will pull down my barns, and build greater; and there will I bestow all my fruits and my goods.

4 And I will say to my soul, Soul, thou hast much goods laid up for many years; take thine ease, eat, drink, *and* be merry.

5 But God said unto him, *Thou* fool, this night thy soul shall be required of thee: then whose shall those things be, which thou hast provided?

6 So *is* he that layeth up treasure for himself, and is not rich toward God.

XVI.

Precepts.

AND he said unto his disciples, Therefore I say unto you, Take no thought for your life, what ye shall eat; neither for the body, what ye shall put on.

2 The life is more than meat, and the body *is more* than raiment.

3 Consider the ravens: for they neither sow nor reap; which neither have storehouse nor barn; and God feedeth them: how much more are ye better than the fowls?

4 And which of you with taking thought can add to his stature one cubit?

5 If ye then be not able to do that thing which is least, why take ye thought for the rest?

6 Consider the lilies how they grow; they toil not, they spin not; and yet I say unto you, that Solomon in all his glory was not arrayed like one of these.

7 If then God so clothe the grass, which is to-day in the field, and tomorrow is cast into the

oven; how much more *will he clothe* you, O ye of little faith?

8 And seek not ye what ye shall eat, or what ye shall drink, neither be ye of doubtful mind.

9 For all these things do the nations of the world seek after: and your Father knoweth that ye have need of these things.

10 But rather seek ye the kingdom of God; and all these things shall be added unto you.

11 Fear not, little flock; for it is your Father's good pleasure to give you the kingdom.

12 Sell that ye have, and give alms; provide yourselves bags which wax not old, a treasure in the heavens that faileth not, where no thief approacheth, neither moth corrupteth.

13 For where your treasure is, there will your heart be also.

14 Let your loins be girded about, and *your* lights burning;

15 And ye yourselves like unto men that wait for their lord, when he will return from the wedding; that when he cometh and knocketh, they may open unto him immediately.

16 Blessed *are* those servants, whom the lord when he cometh shall find watching; verily I say unto you, that he shall gird himself, and make them to sit down to meat, and will come forth and serve them.

17 And if he shall come in the second watch, or come in the third watch, and find *them* so, blessed are those servants.

18 And this know, that if the goodman of the house had known what hour the thief would come, he would have watched, and not have suffered his house to be broken through.

19 Be ye therefore ready also: for the Son of man cometh at an hour when ye think not.

20 ¶ Then Peter said unto him, Lord, speakest thou this parable unto us, or even to all?

21 And the Lord said, Who then is that faithful and wise steward, whom *his* lord shall make ruler over his household, to give *them their* portion of meat in due season?

22 Blessed *is* that servant, whom his lord when he cometh shall find so doing.

23 Of a truth, I say unto you, that he will make him ruler over all that he hath.

24 But and if that servant say in his heart, My
lord delayeth his coming; and shall begin to beat
the menservants and maidens, and to eat and
drink, and to be drunken;

25 The lord of that servant will come in a day
when he looketh not for *him*, and at an hour when
he is not aware, and will cut him in sunder, and
will appoint him his portion with the unbelievers.

26 And that servant, which knew his lord's
will, and prepared not *himself*, neither did according to his will, shall be beaten with many *stripes*.

27 But he that knew not, and did commit
things worthy of stripes, shall be beaten with few
stripes. For unto whomsoever much is given, of
him shall be much required: and to whom men
have committed much, of him they will ask the
more.

28 ¶ And he said also to the people, When ye
see a cloud rise out of the west, straightway ye
say, There cometh a shower; and so it is.

29 And when *ye see* the south wind blow, ye
say, There will be heat; and it cometh to pass.

30 *Ye* hypocrites, ye can discern the face of the
sky and of the earth; but how is it that ye do not
discern this time?

31 Yea, and why even of yourselves judge ye not what is right?

32 ¶ When thou goest with thine adversary to the magistrate, *as thou art* in the way, give diligence that thou mayest be delivered from him; lest he hale thee to the judge, and the judge deliver thee to the officer, and the officer cast thee into prison.

33 I tell thee, thou shalt not depart thence, till thou hast paid the very last mite.

34 There were present at that season some that told him of the Galileans, whose blood Pilate had mingled with their sacrifices.

35 And Jesus answering said unto them, Suppose ye that these Galileans were sinners above all the Galileans, because they suffered such things?

36 I tell you, Nay: but, except ye repent, ye shall all likewise perish.

37 Or those eighteen, upon whom the tower in Siloam fell, and slew them, think ye that they were sinners above all men that dwelt in Jerusalem?

38 I tell you, Nay: but, except ye repent, ye shall all likewise perish.

XVII.

Parable of the Fig Tree.

HE spake also this parable; A certain *man* had a fig tree planted in his vineyard; and he came and sought fruit thereon, and found none.

2   Then said he unto the dresser of his vineyard, Behold, these three years I come seeking fruit on this fig tree, and find none: cut it down; why cumbereth it the ground?

3   And he answering said unto him, Lord, let it alone this year also, till I shall dig about it, and dung *it:*

4   And if it bear fruit, *well:* and if not, *then* after that thou shalt cut it down.

XVIII.

Precepts.

AND as he spake a certain Pharisee besought him to dine with him: and he went in, and sat down to meat.

2 And when the Pharisee saw *it*, he marvelled that he had not first washed before dinner.

3 And the Lord said unto him, Now do ye Pharisees make clean the outside of the cup and the platter; but your inward part is full of ravening and wickedness.

4 *Ye* fools, did not he that made that which is without make that which is within also?

5 But rather give alms of such things as ye have; and, behold, all things are clean unto you.

6 But woe unto you, Pharisees! for ye tithe mint and rue and all manner of herbs, and pass over judgment and the love of God: these ought ye to have done, and not to leave the other undone.

7 Woe unto you, Pharisees! for ye love the uppermost seats in the synagogues, and greetings in the markets.

8 Woe unto you, scribes and Pharisees, hypocrites! for ye are as graves which appear not, and the men that walk over *them* are not aware *of them*.

9 Then answered one of the lawyers, and said unto him, Master, thus saying thou reproachest us also.

10   And he said, Woe unto you also, *ye* lawyers! for ye lade men with burdens grievous to be borne, and ye yourselves touch not the burdens with one of your fingers.

11   Woe unto you, lawyers! for ye have taken away the key of knowledge: ye entered not in yourselves, and them that were entering in ye hindered.

12   And as he said these things unto them, the scribes and the Pharisees began to urge *him* vehemently, and to provoke him to speak of many things:

13   Laying wait for him, and seeking to catch something out of his mouth, that they might accuse him.

XIX.

Parable of the Sower.

THE same day went Jesus out of the house, and sat by the sea side.

2   And great multitudes were gathered together unto him, so that he went into a ship, and sat; and the whole multitude stood on the shore.

3   And he spoke many things unto them in parables, saying, Behold, a sower went forth to sow;

4   And when he sowed, some *seeds* fell by the
way side, and the fowls came and devoured them
up:

5   Some fell upon stony places, where they had
not much earth: and forthwith they sprung up, because they had no deepness of earth:

6   And when the sun was up, they were
scorched; and because they had no root, they withered away.

7   And some fell among thorns; and the thorns
sprung up, and choked them:

8   But other fell into good ground, and brought
forth fruit, some an hundredfold, some sixtyfold,
some thirtyfold.

9   Who hath ears to hear, let him hear.

10   ¶ And when he was alone, they that were
about him with the twelve asked of him the par
able.

11   ¶ Hear ye therefore the parable of the sower.

12   When any one heareth the word of the kingdom, and understandeth *it* not, then cometh the

wicked *one*, and catcheth away that which was sown in his heart. This is he which received seed by the way side.

13 But he that received the seed into stony places, the same is he that heareth the word, and anon with joy receiveth it;

14 Yet hath he not root in himself, but dureth for a while; for when tribulation or persecution ariseth because of the word, by and by he is offended.

15 He also that received seed among the thorns is he that heareth the word; and the care of this world, and the deceitfulness of riches choke the word, and he becometh unfruitful.

16 But he that received seed into the good ground is he that heareth the word, and understandeth *it;* which also beareth fruit, and bringeth forth, some an hundredfold, some sixty, some thirty.

OF JESUS OF NAZARETH.

XX.

Precepts.

A ND he said unto them, Is a candle brought to be put under a bushel, or under a bed? and not to be set on a candlestick?

1 For there is nothing hid, which shall not be manifested; neither was any thing kept secret, but that it should come abroad.

2 If any man have ears to hear, let him hear.

XXI.

Parable of the Tares.

A NOTHER parable put he forth unto them, saying, The kingdom of heaven is likened unto a man which sowed good seed in his field.

2 But while men slept, his enemy came and sowed tares among the wheat, and went his way.

3 But when the blade was sprung up, and brought forth fruit, then appeared the tares also.

4 So the servants of the householder came and said unto him, Sir, didst not thou sow good seed in thy field? from whence then hath it tares?

5 He said unto them, An enemy hath done this. The servants said unto him, Wilt thou then that we go and gather them up?

6 But he said, Nay; lest while ye gather up the tares, ye root up also the wheat with them.

7 Let both grow together until the harvest: and in the time of harvest I will say to the reapers, Gather ye together first the tares, and bind them in bundles to burn them: but gather the wheat into my barn.

8 ¶ Then Jesus sent the multitude away, and went into the house: and his disciples came unto him, saying, Declare unto us the parable of the tares of the field.

9 He answered and said unto them, He that soweth the good seed is the Son of man;

10 The field is the world; the good seed are the children of the kingdom; but the tares are the children of the wicked *one;*

11   The enemy that sowed them is the devil; the harvest is the end of the world; and the reapers are the angels.

12   As therefore the tares are gathered and burned in the fire; so shall it be in the end of this world.

13   The Son of man shall send forth his angels and they shall gather out of his kingdom all things that offend, and them which do iniquity.

14   And shall cast them into a furnace of fire: there shall be wailing and gnashing of teeth.

15   Then shall the righteous shine forth as the sun in the kingdom of their Father.   Who hath ears to hear, let him hear.

16   ¶ Again, the kingdom of heaven is like unto treasure hid in a field; the which when a man hath found, he hideth, and for joy thereof goeth and selleth all that he hath, and buyeth that field.

17   ¶ Again, the kingdom of heaven is like unto a merchant man, seeking goodly pearls:

18   Who, when he had found one pearl of great price, went and sold all that he had, and bought it.

19 ¶ Again, the kingdom of heaven is like unto a net, that was cast into the sea, and gathered of every kind:

20 Which, when it was full, they drew to shore, and sat down, and gathered the good into vessels, but cast the bad away.

21 So shall it be at the end of the world: the angels shall come forth, and sever the wicked from among the just,

22 And shall cast them into the furnace of fire: there shall be wailing and gnashing of teeth.

23 Jesus saith unto them, Have ye understood all these things? They say unto him, Yea, Lord.

24 Then said he unto them, Therefore every scribe *which is* instructed unto the kingdom of heaven is like unto a man *that is* an householder, which bringeth forth out of his treasure *things* new and old.

XXII.

Precepts.

A ND he said, So is the kingdom of God, as if a
man should cast seed into the ground;

2 And should sleep, and rise night and day,
and the seed should spring and grow up, he knoweth not how.

3 For the earth bringeth forth fruit of herself;
first the blade, then the ear, after that the full corn
in the ear.

4 But when the fruit is brought forth, immediately he putteth in the sickle, because the harvest
is come.

5 ¶ And he said, Whereunto shall we liken the
kingdom of God? or with what comparison shall
we compare it?

6 *It is* like a grain of mustard seed, which, when
it is sown in the earth, is less than all the seeds
that be in the earth:

7 But when it is sown, it groweth up, and becometh greater than all herbs, and shooteth out
great branches; so that the fowls of the air may
lodge under the shadow of it.

5

8 And with many such parables spake he the word unto them, as they were able to hear *it*.

9 But without a parable spake he not unto them; and when they were alone, he expounded all things to his disciples.

10 ¶ And it came to pass, that, as they went in the way, a certain *man* said unto him, Lord, I will follow thee whithersoever thou goest.

11 And Jesus said unto him, Foxes have holes, and birds of the air *have* nests; but the Son of man hath not where to lay *his* head.

12 And he said unto another, Follow me. But he said, Lord, suffer me first to go and bury my father.

13 Jesus said unto him, Let the dead bury their dead: but go thou and preach the kingdom of God.

14 And another also said, Lord, I will follow thee; but let me first go bid them farewell, which are at home at my house.

15 And Jesus said unto him, No man, having put his hand to the plough and looking back, is fit for the kingdom of God.

16 ¶ And after these things he went forth, and saw a publican named Levi, sitting at the receipt of custom: and he said unto him, Follow me.

17   And he left all, rose up, and followed him.

18   And Levi made him a great feast in his own house; and it came to pass, that, as Jesus sat at meat in his house, many publicans and sinners sat also together with Jesus and his disciples: for there were many, and they followed him.

19   And when the scribes and Pharisees saw him eat with publicans and sinners, they said unto his disciples, How is it that he eateth and drinketh with publicans and sinners?

20   When Jesus heard *it*, he saith unto them, They that are whole have no need of the physician, but they that are sick: I came not to call the righteous, but sinners to repentance.

XXIII.

Parable of New Wine in Old Bottles.

AND he spake also a parable unto them; No man putteth a piece of a new garment upon an old; if otherwise, then both the new maketh a rent, and the piece that was *taken* out of the new agreeth not with the old.

2   And no man putteth new wine into old bottles; else the new wine will burst the bottles, and be spilled and the bottles shall perish.

3   But new wine must be put into new bottles; and both are preserved.

4   No man also having drunk old *wine* straightway desireth new: for he saith, The old is better.

XXIV.

A Prophet Hath no Honor in his Own Country.

AND it came to pass, *that* when Jesus had finished these parables, he departed thence.

2   And when he was come into his own country, he taught them in their synagogue, insomuch that they were astonished and said, Whence hath this *man* this wisdom, and *these* mighty works?

3   Is not this the carpenter's son? is not his mother called Mary? and his brethren James, and Joses, and Simon, and Judas?

4   And his sisters, are they not all with us? Whence then hath this *man* all these things?

5 And they were offended in him. But Jesus said unto them, A prophet is not without honour, save in his own country, and in his own house.

XXV.

Mission Instructions, Return of Apostles.

B UT when he saw the multitudes, he was moved with compassion on them, because they fainted and were scattered abroad, as sheep having no shepherd.

2 ¶ And he called *unto him* the twelve, and be-gan to send them forth by two and two; and gave them power over unclean spirits;

3 These twelve Jesus sent forth, and com-manded them, saying, Go not into the way of the Gentiles, and into *any* city of the Samaritans enter ye not:

4 But go rather to the lost sheep of the house of Israel.

5 Provide neither gold, nor silver, nor brass in your purses,

6 Nor scrip for *your* journey, neither two coats, neither shces, nor yet staves: for the workman is worthy of his meat.

7 And into whatsoever city or town ye shall enter, enquire who in it is worthy; and there abide till ye go thence.

8 And when you come into an house, salute it.

9 And if the house be worthy, let your peace come upon it: but if it be not worthy, let your peace return to you.

10 And whosoever shall not receive you, nor hear your words, when ye depart out of that house or city, shake off the dust of your feet.

11 Verily I say unto you, It shall be more toler-able for the land of Sodom and Gomorrah in the day of judgment, than for that city.

12 ¶ Behold, I send you forth as sheep in the midst of wolves: be ye therefore wise as serpents, and harmless as doves.

13 But beware of men: for they will deliver you up to the councils, and they will scourge you in their synagogues;

14 And ye shall be brought before governors and kings for my sake, for a testimony against them and the Gentiles.

15 But when they persecute you in this city, flee ye into another: for verily I say unto you, Ye shall not have gone over the cities of Israel, till the Son of man be come.

16 Fear them not therefore: for there is nothing covered, that shall not be revealed; and hid, that shall not be known.

17 What I tell you in darkness, *that* speak ye in light: and what ye hear in the ear, that preach ye upon the housetops.

18 And fear not them which kill the body, but are not able to kill the soul: but rather fear him which is able to destroy both soul and body in hell.

19 Are not two sparrows sold for a farthing? and one of them shall not fall on the ground without your Father.

20 But the very hairs of your head are all numbered.

21 Fear ye not therefore, ye are of more value than many sparrows.

22   And they went out, and preached that men should repent.

23   ¶ And the apostles gathered themselves to-gether unto Jesus, and told him all things, both what they had done, and what they had taught.

XXVI.

Precepts.

AFTER these things Jesus walked in Galilee: for he would not walk in Jewry, because the Jews sought to kill him.

2   Then came together unto him the Pharisees, and certain of the scribes, which came from Jeru-salem.

3   And when they saw some of his disciples eat bread with defiled, that is to say, with unwashen, hands, they found fault.

4   For the Pharisees, and all the Jews, except they wash *their* hands oft, eat not, holding the tra-dition of the elders.

5   And *when they come* from the market, except they wash, they eat not.   And many other things

there be, which they have received to hold, *as* the washing of cups and pots, brazen vessels, and of tables.

6 Then the Pharisees and scribes asked him, Why walk not thy disciples according to the tradition of the elders, but eat bread with unwashen hands?

7 ¶ And when he had called all the people *unto him,* he said unto them, Hearken unto me every one *of you,* and understand:

8 There is nothing from without a man, that entering into him can defile him: but the things which come out of him, those are they that defile the man.

9 If any man have ears to hear let him hear.

10 And when he was entered into the house from the people, his disciples asked him concerning the parable.

11 And he saith unto them, Are ye so without understanding also? Do ye not perceive, that whatsoever thing from without entereth into the man, *it* cannot defile him;

12   Because it entereth not into his heart, but into the belly, and goeth out into the draught, purging all meats?

13   And he said, That which cometh out of the man, that defileth the man.

14   For from within, out of the heart of men, proceed evil thoughts, adulteries, fornications, murders,

15   Thefts, covetousness, wickedness, deceit, lasciviousness, an evil eye, blasphemy, pride, foolishness:

16   All these evil things come from within, and defile the man.

17   ¶ And from thence he aróse, and went into the borders of Tyre and Sidon, and entered into an house, and would have no man know *it:* but he could not be hid.

18   At the same time came the disciples unto Jesus, saying, Who is the greatest in the kingdom of heaven?

19   And Jesus called a little child unto him, and set him in the midst of them,

20 And said, Verily I say unto you, Except ye be converted, and become as little children, ye shall not enter into the kingdom of heaven.

21 Whosoever therefore shall humble himself as this little child, the same is greatest in the kingdom of heaven.

22 ¶ Woe unto the world because of offences! for it must needs be that offences come; but woe to that man by whom the offence cometh!

23 Wherefore if thy hand or thy foot offend thee, cut them off, and cast *them* from thee: it is better for thee to enter into life halt or maimed, rather than having two hands or two feet to be cast into everlasting fire.

24 And if thine eye offend thee, pluck it out, and cast *it* from thee: it is better for thee to enter into life with one eye, rather than having two eyes to be cast into hell fire.

25 How think ye? if a man have an hundred sheep, and one of them be gone astray, doth he not leave the ninety and nine, and goeth into the mountains, and seeketh that which is gone astray?

26 And if so be that he find it, verily I say unto you, he rejoiceth more of that *sheep*, than of the ninety and nine which went not astray.

27 Even so it is not the will of your Father which is in heaven, that one of these little ones should perish.

28 Moreover if thy brother shall trespass against thee, go and tell him his fault between thee and him alone: if he shall hear thee, thou hast gained thy brother.

29 But if he will not hear *thee, then* take with thee one or two more, that in the mouth of two or three witnesses every word may be established.

30 And if he shall neglect to hear them, tell *it* unto the church: but if he neglect to hear the church, let him be unto thee as an heathen man and a publican.

31 ¶ Then came Peter to him, and said, Lord, how oft shall my brother sin against me, and I forgive him? till seven times?

32 Jesus saith unto him, I say not unto thee, Until seven times: but, Until seventy times seven.

XXVII.

Parable of the Wicked Servant.

THEREFORE is the kingdom of heaven likened unto a certain king, which would take account of his servants.

2 And when he had begun to reckon, one was brought unto him, which owed him ten thousand talents.

3 But forasmuch as he had not to pay, his lord commanded him to be sold, and his wife, and children, and all that he had, and payment to be made.

4 The servant therefore fell down, and worshipped him, saying, Lord, have patience with me, and I will pay thee all.

5 Then the lord of that servant was moved with compassion, and loosed him, and forgave him the debt.

6 But the same servant went out, and found one of his fellow-servants, which owed him an hundred pence: and he laid hands on him, and took *him* by the throat, saying, Pay me that thou owest.

7 And his fellow-servant fell down at his feet, and besought him, saying, Have patience with me, and I will pay thee all.

8 And he would not: but went and cast him into prison, till he should pay the debt.

9 So when his fellow-servants saw what was done, they were very sorry, and came and told unto their lord all that was done.

10 Then his lord, after that he had called him, said unto him, O thou wicked servant, I forgave thee all that debt, because thou desiredst me;

11 Shouldest not thou also have had compassion on thy fellow-servant, even as I had pity on thee?

12 And his lord was wroth, and delivered him to the tormentors, till he should pay all that was due unto him.

13 So likewise shall my heavenly Father do also unto you, if ye from your hearts forgive not every one his brother their trespasses.

XXVIII.

Mission of the Seventy.

AFTER these things the Lord appointed other seventy also, and sent them two and two before his face into every city and place, whither he himself would come.

2 Therefore said he unto them, The harvest truly *is* great, but the labourers *are* few: pray ye therefore the Lord of the harvest, that he would send forth labourers into his harvest.

3 Go your ways: behold, I send you forth as lambs among wolves.

4 Carry neither purse, nor scrip, nor shoes: and salute no man by the way.

5 And into whatsoever house ye enter, first say, Peace *be* to this house.

6 And if the son of peace be there, your peace shall rest upon it: if not, it shall turn to you again.

7 And in the same house remain, eating and drinking such things as they give: for the labourer is worthy of his hire. Go not from house to house.

8 And into whatsoever city ye enter, and they receive you, eat such things as are set before you:

9 But into whatsoever city ye enter, and they receive you not, go your ways out into the streets of the same, and say,

10 Even the very dust of your city, which cleaveth on us, we do wipe off against you: notwithstanding be ye sure of this, that the kingdom of God is come nigh unto you.

11 But I say unto you, that it shall be more tolerable in that day for Sodom, than for that city.

XXIX.

The Feast of the Tabernacles.

NOW the Jews' feast of tabernacles was at hand.
   2 His brethren therefore said unto him, Depart hence, and go into Judea, that thy disciples also may see the works that thou doest.

3 For *there is* no man *that* doeth any thing in secret and he himself seeketh to be known openly. If thou do these things, shew thyself to the world.

4 For neither did his brethren believe in him.

5 Then Jesus said unto them, My time is not yet come: but your time is alway ready.

6 The world cannot hate you; but me it hateth, because I testify of it, that the works thereof are evil.

7 Go ye up unto this feast: I go not up yet unto this feast; for my time is not yet full come.

8 When he had said these words unto them, he abode *still* in Galilee.

9 ¶ But when his brethren were gone up, then went he also up unto the feast, not openly, but as it were in secret.

10 Then the Jews sought him at the feast, and said, Where is he?

11 And there was much murmuring among the people concerning him: for some said, He is a good man: others said, Nay; but he deceiveth the people.

12 Howbeit no man spake openly of him for fear of the Jews.

13 ¶ Now about the midst of the feast Jesus went up into the temple, and taught.

14 And the Jews marveled, saying, How knoweth this man letters, having never learned?

15 Jesus answered them, and said, My doctrine is not mine, but his that sent me.

6

16 Did not Moses give you the law, and *yet* none of you keepeth the law? Why go ye about to kill me?

17 The people answered and said, Thou hast a devil: who goeth about to kill thee?

18 Jesus answered and said unto them, I have done one work, and ye all marvel.

19 Moses therefore gave unto you circumcision; (not because it is of Moses, but of the fathers;) and ye on the sabbath day circumcise a man.

20 If a man on the sabbath day receive circumcision, that the law of Moses should not be broken; are ye angry at me, because I have made a man every whit whole cn the sabbath day?

21 Judge not according to the appearance, but judge righteous judgment.

22 Then said some of them of Jerusalem, Is not this he, whom they seek to kill?

23 But, lo, he speaketh boldly, and they say nothing unto him. Do the rulers know indeed that this is the very Christ?

24 ¶ The Pharisees heard that the people murmured such things concerning him; and the Pharisees and the chief priests sent officers to take him.

25 So there was a division among the people because of him.

26 And some of them would have taken him; but no man laid hands on him.

27 ¶ Then came the officers to the chief priests and Pharisees; and they said unto them, Why have ye not brought him?

28 The officers answered, Never man spake like this man.

29 Then answered them the Pharisees, Are ye also deceived?

30 Have any of the rulers or of the Pharisees believed on him?

31 But this people who knoweth not the law are cursed.

32 Nicodemus saith unto them, (he that came to Jesus by night, being one of them,)

33 Doth our law judge *any* man, before it hear him, and know what he doeth?

34 They answered and said unto him, Art thou also of Galilee? Search, and look: for out of Galilee ariseth no prophet.

35 And every man went unto his own house.

XXX.

The Woman Taken in Adultery.

J ESUS went unto the mount of Olives.

2   And early in the morning he came again into the temple, and all the people came unto him; and he sat down, and taught them.

3   And the scribes and Pharisees brought unto him a woman taken in adultery; and when they had set her in the midst,

4   They say unto him, Master, this woman was taken in adultery, in the very act.

5   Now Moses in the law commanded us, that such should be stoned; but what sayest thou?

6   This they said, tempting him, that they might have to accuse him. But Jesus stooped down, and with *his* finger wrote on the ground, *as though he heard them not.*

7   So when they continued asking him, he lifted up himself, and said unto them, He that is without sin among you, let him first cast a stone at her.

8   And again he stooped down, and wrote on the ground.

9   And they which heard *it*, being convicted by *their own* conscience, went out one by one beginning at the eldest, *even* unto the last: and Jesus was left alone, and the woman standing in the midst.

10   When Jesus had lifted up himself, and saw none but the woman, he said unto her, Woman, where are those thine accusers? hath no man condemned thee?

11   She said, No man, Lord.   And Jesus said unto her, Neither do I condemn thee; go, and sin no more.

XXXI.

To be Born Blind No Proof of Sin.

AND as *Jesus* passed by, he saw a man which was blind from *his* birth.

2   And his disciples asked him, saying, Master, who did sin, this man, or his parents, that he was born blind?

3   Jesus answered, Neither hath this man sinned, nor his parents: but that the works of God should be made manifest in him.

XXXII.

The Good Shepherd.

VERILY, verily, I say unto you, He that entereth not by the door into the sheepfold, but climbeth up some other way, the same is a thief and a robber.

2 But he that entereth in by the door is the shepherd of the sheep.

3 To him the porter openeth; and the sheep hear his voice: and he calleth his own sheep by name, and leadeth them out.

4 And when he putteth forth his own sheep, he goeth before them, and the sheep follow him; for they know his voice.

5 And a stranger will they not follow, but will flee from him: for they know not the voice of strangers.

6 I am the good shepherd: the good shepherd giveth his life for the sheep.

7 But he that is an hireling, and not the shepherd, whose own the sheep are not, seeth the wolf coming, and leaveth the sheep, and fleeth: and the wolf catcheth them, and scattereth the sheep.

8　The hireling fleeth, because he is an hireling, and careth not for the sheep.

9　I am the good shepherd, and know my *sheep*, and am known of mine.

10　And other sheep I have, which are not of this fold: them also I must bring, and they shall hear my voice; and there shall be one fold, *and* one shepherd.

XXXIII.

Love God and Thy Neighbour; Parable of the Samaritan.

AND, behold, a certain lawyer stood up, and tempted him, saying, Master, what shall I do to inherit eternal life?

2　He said unto him, What is written in the law? how readest thou?

3　And he answering said, Thou shalt love the Lord thy God with all thy heart, and with all thy soul, and with all thy strength, and with all thy mind; and thy neighbour as thyself.

4　And he said unto him, Thou hast answered right: this do, and thou shalt live.

5   But he, willing to justify himself, said unto Jesus, And who is my neighbour?

6   And Jesus answering said, A certain *man* went down from Jerusalem to Jericho, and fell among thieves, which stripped him of his raiment, and wounded *him*, and departed, leaving *him* half dead.

7   And by chance there came down a certain priest that way: and when he saw him he passed by on the other side.

8   And likewise a Levite, when he was at the place, came and looked *on him*, and passed by on the other side.

9   But a certain Samaritan, as he journeyed, came where he was: and when he saw him, he had compassion *on him*,

10   And went to *him*, and bound up his wounds, pouring in oil and wine, and set him on his own beast, and brought him to an inn, and took care of him.

11   And on the morrow when he departed, he took out two pence, and gave *them* to the host, and said unto him, Take care of him; and whatsoever thou spendest more, when I come again, I will repay thee.

12 Which now of these three, thinkest thou, was neighbour unto him that fell among the thieves?

13 And he said, He that shewed mercy on him. Then said Jesus unto him, Go, and do thou likewise.

XXXIV.

Form of Prayer.

A ND it came to pass, that, as he was praying in a certain place, when he ceased, one of his disciples said unto him, Lord, teach us to pray, as John also taught his disciples.

2 And he said unto them, When ye pray, say, Our Father which art in heaven, Hallowed be thy name. Thy kingdom come. Thy will be done, as in heaven, so in earth.

3 Give us day by day our daily bread.

4 And forgive us our sins; for we also forgive every one that is indebted to us. And lead us not into temptation; but deliver us from evil.

5 And he said unto them, Which of you shall have a friend, and shall go unto him at midnight, and say unto him, Friend, lend me three loaves;

6 For a friend of mine in his journey is come to me, and I have nothing to set before him?

7 And he from within shall answer and say, Trouble me not: the door is now shut; and my children are with me in bed; I cannot rise and give thee.

8 I say unto you, Though he will not rise and give him because he is his friend, yet because of his importunity he will rise and give him as many as he needeth.

9 And I say unto you, Ask, and it shall be given you; seek, and ye shall find; knock, and it shall be opened unto you.

10 For every one that asketh receiveth; and he that seeketh findeth; and to him that knocketh it shall be opened.

11 If a son shall ask bread of any of you that is a father, will he give him a stone? or if *he ask* a fish, will he for a fish give him a serpent?

12 Or if he shall ask an egg, will he offer him a scorpion?

13 If ye then, being evil, know how to give good gifts unto your children: how much more shall *your* heavenly Father give the Holy Spirit to them that ask him?

XXXV.

The Sabbath.

A ND it came to pass, as he went into the house of one of the chief Pharisees to eat bread on the sabbath day, that they watched him.

2 And, behold, there was a certain man before him which had the dropsy.

3 And Jesus answering spake unto the lawyers and Pharisees, saying, Is it lawful to heal on the sabbath day?

4 And they held their peace. And he took *him*, and healed him, and let him go;

5 And answered them, saying, Which of you shall have an ass or an ox fallen into a pit, and will not straightway pull him out on the sabbath day?

6 And they could not answer him again to these things.

XXXVI.

The Bidden to a Feast.

AND he put forth a parable to those which were bidden, when he marked how they chose out the chief rooms; saying unto them,

2   When thou art bidden of any *man* to a wedding, sit not down in the highest room; lest a more honourable man than thou be bidden of him;

3   And he that bade thee and him come and say to thee, Give this man place; and thou begin with shame to take the lowest room.

4   But when thou art bidden, go and sit down in the lowest room; that when he that bade thee cometh, he may say unto thee, Friend, go up higher: then shalt thou have worship in the presence of them that sit at meat with thee.

5   For whosoever exalteth himself shall be abased; and he that humbleth himself shall be exalted.

6   ¶ Then said he also to him that bade him, When thou makest a dinner or a supper, call not

thy friends, nor thy brethren, neither thy kinsmen, nor *thy* rich neighbours; lest they also bid thee again, and a recompense be made thee.

7   But when thou makest a feast, call the poor, the maimed, the lame, the blind:

8   And thou shalt be blessed; for they cannot recompense thee: for thou shalt be recompensed at the resurrection of the just.

9   ¶ And when one of them that sat at meat with him heard these things, he said unto him, Blessed *is* he that shall eat bread in the kingdom of God.

10   Then said he unto him, A certain man made a great supper, and bade many:

11   And sent his servant at supper time to say to them that were bidden, Come; for all things are now ready.

12   And they all with one *consent* began to make excuse.   The first said unto him, I have bought a piece of ground, and I must needs go and see it: I pray thee have me excused.

13   And another said, I have bought five yoke of oxen, and I go to prove them: I pray thee have me excused.

14   And another said, I have married a wife, and therefore I cannot come.

15   So that servant came, and shewed his lord these things.   Then the master of the house being angry said to his servant, Go out quickly into the streets and lanes of the city, and bring in hither the poor, and the maimed, and the halt, and the blind.

16   And the servant said, Lord it is done as thou hast commanded, and yet there is room.

17   And the lord said unto the servant, Go out into the highways and hedges, and compel *them* to come in, that my house may be filled.

18   For 1 say unto you, That none of those men which were bidden shall taste of my supper.

XXXVII.

Precepts.

FOR which of you, intending to build a tower, sitteth not down first, and counteth the cost, whether he have *sufficient* to finish *it?*

2   Lest haply, after he hath laid the foundation, and is not able to finish *it*, all that behold *it* begin to mock him,

3   Saying, This man began to build, and was not able to finish.

4   Or what king, going to make war against another king, sitteth not down first, and consulteth whether he be able with ten thousand to meet him that cometh against him with twenty thousand?

5   Or else, while the other is yet a great way off, he sendeth an ambassage, and desireth conditions of peace.

XXXVIII.

Parables of the Lost Sheep and Prodigal Son.

THEN drew near unto him all the publicans and sinners for to hear him.

2   And the Pharisees and scribes murmured, saying, This man receiveth sinners, and eateth with them.

3   And he spake this parable unto them, saying,

4   What man of you, having an hundred sheep, if he lose one of them, doth not leave the ninety and nine in the wilderness, and go after that which is lost, until he find it?

5   And when he hath found *it*, he layeth *it* on his shoulders, rejoicing.

6   And when he cometh home, he calleth together *his* friends and neighbours, saying unto them, Rejoice with me; for I have found my sheep which was lost.

7   I say unto you, that likewise joy shall be in heaven over one sinner that repenteth, more than over ninety and nine just persons, which need no repentance.

8   ¶ Either what woman having ten pieces of silver, if she lose one piece, doth not light a candle, and sweep the house, and seek diligently till she find *it?*

9   And when she hath found *it*, she calleth *her* friends and *her* neighbours together, saying, Rejoice with me; for I have found the piece which I had lost.

10   Likewise, I say unto you, there is joy in the presence of the angels of God over one sinner that repenteth.

11 ¶ And he said, A certain man had two sons:

12 And the younger of them said to *his* father, Father, give me the portion of goods that falleth *to me*. And he divided unto them *his* living.

13 And not many days after the younger son gathered all together and took his journey into a far country, and there wasted his substance with riotous living.

14 And when he had spent all, there arose a mighty famine in that land; and he began to be in want.

15 And he went and joined himself to a citizen of that country; and he sent him into his fields to feed swine.

16 And he would fain have filled his belly with the husks that the swine did eat: and no man gave unto him.

17 And when he came to himself, he said, How many hired servants of my father's have bread enough and to spare, and I perish with hunger!

18 I will arise and go to my father, and will say unto him, Father, I have sinned against heaven, and before thee,

7

19   And am no more worthy to be called thy son: make me as one of thy hired servants.

20   And he arose, and came to his father. But when he was yet a great way off, his father saw him, and had compassion, and ran, and fell on his neck, and kissed him.

21   And the son said unto him, Father, I have sinned against heaven, and in thy sight, and am no more worthy to be called thy son.

22   But the father said to his servants, Bring forth the best robe, and put *it* on him; and put a ring on his hand, and shoes on *his* feet:

23   And bring hither the fatted calf, and kill *it;* and let us eat, and be merry:

24   For this my son was dead, and is alive again; he was lost, and is found. And they began to be merry.

25   Now his elder son was in the field; and as he came and drew nigh to the house, he heard music and dancing.

26   And he called one of the servants, and asked what these things meant.

27   And he said unto him, Thy brother is come; and thy father hath killed the fatted calf, because he hath received him safe and sound.

28 And he was angry, and would not go in: therefore came his father out, and intreated him.

29 And he answering said to *his* father, Lo, these many years do I serve thee, neither transgressed I at any time thy commandment: and yet thou never gavest me a kid, that I might make merry with my friends:

30 But as soon as this thy son was come, which hath devoured thy living with harlots, thou hast killed for him the fatted calf.

31 And he said unto him, Son, thou art ever with me, and all that I have is thine.

32 It was meet that we should make merry, and be glad; for this thy brother was dead, and is alive again; and was lost, and is found.

XXXIX.

Parable of the Unjust Steward.

AND he said also unto his disciples, There was a certain rich man, which had a steward; and the same was accused unto him that he had wasted his goods.

2   And he called him, and said unto him, How is it that I hear this of thee? give an account of thy stewardship; for thou mayest be no longer steward.

3   Then the steward said within himself, What shall I do? for my lord taketh away from me the stewardship: I cannot dig; to beg I am ashamed.

4   I am resolved what to do, that, when I am put out of the stewardship, they may receive me into their houses.

5   So he called every one of his lord's debtors *unto him,* and said unto the first, How much owest thou unto my lord?

6   And he said, An hundred measures of oil. And he said unto him, Take thy bill, and sit down quickly, and write fifty.

7   Then said he to another, And how much owest thou?   And he said, An hundred measures of wheat.   And he said unto him, Take thy bill, and write fourscore.

8   And the lord commended the unjust steward, because he had done wisely; for the children of this world are in their generation wiser than the children of light.

9 And I say unto you, Make to yourselves friends of the mammon of unrighteousness; that, when ye fail, they may receive you into everlasting habitations.

10 He that is faithful in that which is least is faithful also in much: and he that is unjust in the least is unjust also in much.

11 If therefore ye have not been faithful in the unrighteous mammon, who will commit to your trust the true *riches?*

12 And if ye have not been faithful in that which is another man's, who shall give you that which is your own?

13 No servant can serve two masters: for either he will hate the one, and love the other; or else he will hold to the one, and despise the other. Ye cannot serve God and mammon.

14 ¶ And the Pharisees also, who were covetous, heard all these things: and they derided him.

15 And he said unto them, Ye are they which justify yourselves before men; but God knoweth your hearts: for that which is highly esteemed among men is abomination in the sight of God.

XL.

Parable of Lazarus.

THERE was a certain rich man, which was clothed in purple and fine linen and fared sumptuously every day:

2   And there was a certain beggar named Lazarus, which was laid at his gate, full of sores,

3   And desiring to be fed with the crumbs which fell from the rich man's table: moreover the dogs came and licked his sores.

4   And it came to pass, that the beggar died, and was carried by the angels into Abraham's bosom: the rich man also died, and was buried;

5   And in hell he lift up his eyes, being in torments and seeth Abraham afar off, and Lazarus in his bosom.

6   And he cried and said, Father Abraham, have mercy on me, and send Lazarus, that he may dip the tip of his finger in water, and cool my tongue; for I am tormented in this flame.

7   But Abraham said, Son, remember that thou in thy lifetime receivedst thy good things, and like-

wise Lazarus evil things: but now he is comforted, and thou art tormented.

8 And beside all this, between us and you there is a great gulf fixed: so that they which would pass from hence to you cannot; neither can they pass to us, that *would come* from thence.

9 Then he said, I pray thee therefore, father, that thou wouldest send him to my father's house:

10 For I have five brethren; that he may testify unto them, lest they also come into this place of torment.

11 Abraham saith unto him, They have Moses and the prophets; let them hear them.

12 And he said, Nay, father Abraham: but if one went unto them from the dead, they will repent.

13 And he said unto him, If they hear not Moses and the prophets, neither will they be persuaded, though one rose from the dead.

XLI.

Precepts to be Always Ready.

THEN said he unto the disciples, it is impossible but that offences will come: but woe *unto him*, through whom they come!

2   It were better for him that a millstone were hanged about his neck, and he cast into the sea, than that he should offend one of these little ones.

3   ¶ Take heed to yourselves: If thy brother trespass against thee, rebuke him; and if he repent, forgive him.

4   And if he trespass against thee seven times in a day, and seven times in a day turn again to thee. saying, I repent; thou shalt forgive him.

5   But which of you, having a servant plowing or feeding cattle, will say unto him by and by, when he is come from the field, Go and sit down to meat?

6   And will not rather say unto him, Make ready wherewith I may sup, and gird thyself, and serve me, till I have eaten and drunken; and afterward thou shalt eat and drink?

7   Doth he thank that servant because he did the things that were commanded him?   I trow not.

8   So likewise ye, when ye shall have done all those things which are commanded you, say, We are unprofitable servants: we have done that which was our duty to do.

9   ¶ And when he was demanded of the Pharisees, when the kingdom of God should come, he

answered them and said, The Kingdom of God cometh not with observation.

10 And as it was in the days of Noe, so shall it be also in the days of the Son of man.

11 They did eat, they drank, they married wives, they were given in marriage, until the day that Noe entered into the ark, and the flood came, and destroyed them all.

12 Likewise also as it was in the days of Lot; they did eat, they drank, they bought, they sold, they planted, they builded;

13 But the same day that Lot went out of Sodom it rained fire and brimstone from heaven, and destroyed *them* all.

14 Even thus shall it be in the day when the Son of man is revealed.

15 In that day, he which shall be upon the housetop, and his staff in the house, let him not come down to take it away: and he that is in the field, let him likewise not return back.

16 Remember Lot's wife.

17 Whosoever shall seek to save his life shall lose it; and whosoever shall lose his life shall preserve it.

18   I tell you, in that night there shall be two *men* in one bed; the one shall be taken, and the other shall be left.

19   Two *women* shall be grinding together; the one shall be taken, and the other left.

20   Two *men* shall be in the field; the one shall be taken, and the other left.

XLII.

Parables of the Widow and Judge, the Pharisee and Publican.

AND he spake a parable unto them *to this end,* that men ought always to pray, and not to faint;

2   Saying, There was in a city a judge, which feared not God, neither regarded man:

3   And there was a widow in that city; and she came unto him, saying, Avenge me of mine adversary.

4   And he would not for a while: but afterward he said within himself, Though I fear not God, nor regard man,

5   Yet because this widow troubleth me, I will avenge her, lest by her continual coming she weary me.

6 And the Lord said, Hear what the unjust judge saith.

7 And shall not God avenge his own elect, which cry day and night unto him, though he bear long with them?

8 I tell you that he will avenge them speedily. Nevertheless when the Son of man cometh, shall he find faith on the earth?

9 ¶ And he spake this parable unto certain which trusted in themselves that they were righteous, and despised others:

10 Two men went up into the temple to pray; the one a Pharisee, and the other a publican.

11 The Pharisee stood and prayed thus with himself, God, I thank thee that I am not as other men *are*, extortioners, unjust, adulterers, or even as this publican.

12 I fast twice in the week, I give tithes of all that I possess.

13 And the publican, standing afar off, would not lift up so much as *his* eyes unto heaven, but smote upon his breast, saying, God be merciful to me a sinner.

14   I tell you, this man went down to his house justified *rather* than the other: for every one that exalteth himself shall be abased; and he that humbleth himself shall be exalted.

XLIII.

Precepts.

NOW it came to pass, as they went, that he entered into a certain village: and a certain woman named Martha received him into her house.

2   And she had a sister called Mary, which also sat at Jesus' feet, and heard his word.

3   But Martha was cumbered about much serving, and came to him, and said, Lord, dost thou not care that my sister hath left me to serve alone? bid her therefore that she help me.

4   And Jesus answered and said unto her, Martha, Martha, thou art careful and troubled about many things:

5   But one thing is needful: and Mary hath chosen that good part, which shall not be taken away from her.

6   And it came to pass, *that* when Jesus had finished these sayings, he departed from Galilee, and came into the coasts of Judea beyond Jordan;

7   And great multitudes followed him; and he healed them there.

8   The Pharisees also came unto him, tempting him, and saying unto him, Is it lawful for a man to put away his wife for every cause?

9   And he answered and said unto them, Have ye not read, that he which made *them* at the beginning made them male and female,

10   And said, For this cause shall a man leave father and mother, and shall cleave to his wife: and they twain shall be one flesh?

11   Wherefore they are no more twain, but one flesh.   What therefore God hath joined together, let not man put asunder.

12   They say unto him, Why did Moses then·command to give a writing of divorcement, and to put her away?

13   He saith unto them, Moses because of the hardness of your hearts suffered you to put away your wives: but from the beginning it was not so.

14 And I say unto you, Whosoever shall put away his wife, except *it be* for fornication, and shall marry another, committeth adultery: and whoso marrieth her which is put away doth commit adultery.

15 His disciples say unto him, If the case of the man be so with *his* wife, it is not good to marry.

16 But he said unto them, All *men* cannot receive this saying, save *they* to whom it is given.

17 For there are some eunuchs, which were so born from *their* mother's womb: and there are some eunuchs, which were made eunuchs of men; and there be eunuchs, which have made themselves eunuchs for the kingdom of heaven's sake. He that is able to receive *it*, let him receive *it*.

18 Then were there brought unto him little children, that he should put *his* hands on them, and pray: and the disciples rebuked them.

19 But Jesus said, Suffer little children. and forbid them not, to come unto me: for of such is the kingdom of heaven.

20 And he laid *his* hands on them, and departed thence.

21　And, behold, one came and said unto him, Good Master, what good thing shall I do, that I may have eternal life?

22　And he said unto him, Why callest thou me good? *there is* none good but one, *that is,* God: but if thou wilt enter into life, keep the commandments.

23　He saith unto him, Which? Jesus said, Thou shalt do no murder, Thou shalt not commit adultery, Thou shalt not steal, Thou shalt not bear false witness,

24　Honour thy father and *thy* mother: and, Thou shalt love thy neighbour as thyself.

25　The young man saith unto him, All these things have I kept from my youth up: what lack I yet?

26　Jesus said unto him, If thou wilt be perfect, go *and* sell that thou hast, and give to the poor, and thou shalt have treasure in heaven: and come *and* follow me.

27　But when the young man heard that saying, he went away sorrowful: for he had great possessions.

28　Then said Jesus unto his disciples, Verily I say unto you, That a rich man shall hardly enter into the kingdom of heaven.

29 And again I say unto you, It is easier for a camel to go through the eye of a needle, than for a rich man to enter into the kingdom of God.

30 When his disciples heard *it*, they were exceedingly amazed, saying, Who then can be saved?

31 But Jesus beheld *them*, and said unto them, With men this is impossible; but with God all things are possible.

XLIV.

Parable of the Labourers in the Vineyard.

FOR the kingdom of heaven is like unto a man *that is* an householder, which went out early in the morning to hire labourers into his vineyard.

2 And when he had agreed with the labourers for a penny a day, he sent them into his vineyard.

3 And he went out about the third hour, and saw others standing idle in the marketplace,

4 And said unto them: Go ye also into the vineyard, and whatsoever is right I will give you. And they went their way.

5 Again he went out about the sixth and ninth hour, and did likewise.

6 And about the eleventh hour he went out, and found others standing idle, and saith unto them, Why stand ye here all the day idle?

7 They say unto him, Because no man hath hired us. He saith unto them, Go ye also into the vineyard; and whatsoever is right, *that* shall ye receive.

8 So when even was come, the lord of the vineyard saith unto his steward, Call the labourers, and give them *their* hire, beginning from the last unto the first.

9 And when they came that *were hired* about the eleventh hour, they received every man a penny.

10 But when the first came, they supposed that they should have received more; and they likewise received every man a penny.

11 And when they had received *it*, they murmured against the goodman of the house,

12 Saying, These last have wrought *but* one hour, and thou hast made them equal unto us, which have borne the burden and heat of the day.

8

13 But he answered one of them, and said, Friend, I do thee no wrong; didst thou not agree with me for a penny?

14 Take *that* thine *is* and go thy way: I will give unto this last, even as unto thee.

15 Is it not lawful for me to do what I will with mine own? Is thine eye evil, because I am good?

16 So the last shall be first, and the first last: for many be called, but few chosen.

XLV.

Zacchaeus, and the Parable of the Talents.

AND *Jesus* entered and passed through Jericho.
2. And, behold, *there was* a man named Zacchaeus, which was the chief among the publicans, and he was rich.

3 And he sought to see Jesus who he was; and could not for the press, because he was little of stature.

4 And he ran before, and climbed up into a sycamore tree to see him: for he was to pass that *way*.

5   And when Jesus came to the place, he looked up, and saw him, and said unto him, Zacchaeus, make haste, and come down; for today I must abide at thy house.

6   And he made haste, and came down, and received him joyfully.

7   And when they saw *it*, they all murmured, saying, That he was gone to be guest with a man that is a sinner.

8   And Zacchaeus stood, and said unto the Lord; Behold, Lord, the half of my goods I give to the poor; and if I have taken anything from any man by false accusation, I restore *him* fourfold.

9   And Jesus said unto him, This day is salvation come to this house, forsomuch as he also is a son of Abraham.

10   For the Son of man is come to seek and to save that which was lost.

11   ¶ And as they heard these things, he added and spake a parable, because he was nigh to Jerusalem, and because they thought that the kingdom of God should immediately appear.

12   He said therefore, A certain nobleman went into a far country to receive for himself a kingdom, and to return.

13   And he called his ten servants, and delivered them ten pounds, and said unto them, Occupy till I come.

14   But his citizens hated him, and sent a message after him, saying, We will not have this *man* to reign over us.

15   And it came to pass, that when he was returned, having received the kingdom, then he commanded these servants to be called unto him, to whom he had given the money, that he might know how much every man had gained by trading.

16   Then came the first, saying, Lord, thy pound hath gained ten pounds.

17   And he said unto him, Well, thou good servant: because thou hast been faithful in a very little, have thou authority over ten cities.

18   And the second came, saying, Lord, thy pound hath gained five pounds.

19   And he said likewise to him, Be thou also over five cities.

20 And another came, saying, Lord, behold, *here is* thy pound, which I have kept laid up in a napkin:

21 For I feared thee, because thou art an austere man: thou takest up that thou layedst not down, and reapest that thou didst not sow.

22 And he saith unto him, Out of thine own mouth will I judge thee, *thou* wicked servant. Thou knewest that I was an austere man, taking up that I laid not down, and reaping that I did not sow:

23 Wherefore then gavest not thou my money into the bank, that at my coming I might have required mine own with usury?

24 And he said unto them that stood by, Take from him the pound, and give *it* to him that hath ten pounds.

25 (And they said unto him, Lord, he hath ten pounds.)

26 For I say unto you, That unto every one which hath shall be given; and from him that hath not, even that he hath shall be taken away from him.

27 But those mine enemies which would not that I should reign over them, bring hither, and slay *them* before me.

28 And when he had thus spoken, he went before, ascending up to Jerusalem.

XLVI.

Goes to Jerusalem and Bethany.

AND when they drew nigh unto Jerusalem, and were come to Bethphage, unto the mount of Olives, then sent Jesus two disciples,

2 Saying unto them, Go into the village over against you, and straightway ye shall find an ass tied, and a colt with her: loose *them*, and bring *them* unto me.

3 And if any *man* say ought unto you, ye shall say, The Lord hath need of them; and straightway he will send them.

4 And the disciples went, and did as Jesus commanded them,

5 And brought the ass, and the colt, and put on them their clothes, and they set *him* thereon.

6 And a very great multitude spread their garments in the way; others cut down branches from the trees, and strawed *them* in the way.

7 And when he was come into Jerusalem, all the city was moved, saying, Who is this?

8 The Pharisees therefore said among themselves, Perceive ye how ye prevail nothing? behold, the world is gone after him.

9 And there were certain Greeks among them that came up to worship at the feast:

10 The same came therefore to Philip, which was of Bethsaida of Galilee, and desired him, saying, Sir, we would see Jesus.

11 Philip cometh and telleth Andrew: and again Andrew and Philip tell Jesus.

12 And Jesus answered them, saying, The hour is come, that the Son of man should be glorified.

13 Verily, verily, I say unto you, Except a corn of wheat fall into the ground and die, it abideth alone: but if it die, it bringeth forth much fruit.

14 And he left them, and went out of the city into Bethany; and he lodged there.

XLVII.

The Traders Cast Out from the Temple.

AND on the morrow, when they were come from Bethany, he was hungry:

2 And they came to Jerusalem: and Jesus went into the temple, and began to cast out them that sold and bought in the temple, and overthrew the tables of the money changers, and the seats of them that sold doves;

3 And would not suffer that any man should carry *any* vessel through the temple.

4 And he taught, saying unto them, Is it not written, My house shall be called of all nations the house of prayer? but ye have made it a den of thieves.

5 And the scribes and chief priests heard *it*, and sought how they might destroy him: for they feared him, because all the people was astonished at his doctrine.

6 And when even was come, he went out of the city.

XLVIII.

Parable of the Two Sons.

AND they came again to Jerusalem: and as he was walking in the temple, there came to him the chief priests, and the scribes, and the elders,

2 And they answered Jesus and said, We cannot tell. And he said unto them, Neither tell I you by what authority I do these things.

3 But what think ye? A *certain* man had two sons; and he came to the first, and said, Son, go work today in my vineyard.

4 He answered and said, I will not: but afterward he repented, and went.

5 And he came to the second, and said likewise. And he answered and said I *go*, sir: and went not.

6 Whether of them twain did the will of *his* father? They say unto him, The first. Jesus saith unto them, Verily I say unto you, That the publicans and the harlots go into the kingdom of God before you.

XLIX.

Parable of the Vineyard and Husbandmen.

HEAR another parable: There was a certain householder, which planted a vineyard, and hedged it round about, and digged a wine-press in it, and built a tower, and let it out to husbandmen, and went into a far country:

2 And at the season he sent to the husbandmen a servant, that he might receive from the husbandmen of the fruit of the vineyard.

3 And they caught *him*, and beat him, and sent *him* away empty.

4 And again he sent unto them another servant; and at him they cast stones, and wounded *him* in the head, and sent *him* away shamefully handled.

5 And again he sent another; and him they killed, and many others; beating some, and killing some.

6 Having yet therefore one son, his well-beloved, he sent him also last unto them, saying, They will reverence my son.

7 But those husbandmen said among them-selves, This is the heir; come, let us kill him, and the inheritance shall be ours.

8 And they took him, and killed *him* and cast *him* out of the vineyard.

9 What shall therefore the lord of the vineyard do? he will come and destroy the husbandmen, and will give the vineyard unto others.

10 And when the chief priests and Pharisees had heard his parables, they perceived that he spake of them.

11 But when they sought to lay hands on him, they feared the multitude, because they took him for a prophet.

L.

Parable of the King and the Wedding.

AND Jesus answered and spake unto them again by parables, and said,

2 The kingdom of heaven is like unto a certain king, which made a marriage for his son;

3   And sent forth his servants to call them that were bidden to the wedding; and they would not come.

4   Again, he sent forth other servants, saying, Tell them which are bidden, Behold, I have prepared my dinner; my oxen and *my* fatlings *are* killed, and all things *are* ready: come unto the marriage.

5   But they made light of *it*, and went their ways, one to his farm, another to his merchandise:

6   And the remnant took his servants, and entreated *them* spitefully, and slew *them.*

7   But when the king heard *thereof*, he was wroth: and he sent forth his armies, and destroyed those murderers, and burned up their city.

8   Then saith he to his servants, The wedding is ready, but they which were bidden were not worthy.

9   Go ye therefore into the highways, and as many as ye shall find, bid to the marriage.

10   So those servants went out into the highways, and gathered together all as many as they found, both bad and good; and the wedding was furnished with guests.

11   And when the king came in to see the guests, he saw there a man which had not on a wedding garment:

12   And he saith unto him, Friend, how camest thou in hither not having a wedding garment? And he was speechless.

13   Then the king said to the servants, Bind him hand and foot, and take him away and cast *him* into outer darkness: there shall be weeping and gnashing of teeth.

14   For many are called, but few *are* chosen.

LI.

Tribute, Marriage, Resurrection.

THEN went the Pharisees, and took counsel how they might entangle him in *his* talk.

2   And they sent out unto him their disciples with the Herodians, saying, Master, we know that thou art true, and teachest the way of God in truth, neither carest thou for any *man:* for thou regardest not the person of men.

3   Tell us therefore, What thinkest thou? Is it lawful to give tribute unto Caesar, or not?

4   But Jesus perceived their wickedness, and said, Why tempt ye me, *ye* hypocrites?

5   Shew me the tribute money.   And they brought unto him a penny.

6   And he saith unto them, Whose *is* this image and superscription?

7   They say unto him, Caesar's.   Then saith he unto them, Render therefore unto Caesar the things which are Caesar's; and unto God the things that are God's.

8   When they had heard *these words,* they marvelled, and left him and went their way.

9   The same day came to him the Sadducees, which say that there is no resurrection, and asked him,

10   Saying, Master, Moses said, If a man die, having no children, his brother shall marry his wife, and raise up seed unto his brother.

11   Now there were with us seven brethren: and the first, when he had married a wife, deceased, and, having no issue, left his wife unto his brother:

12   Likewise the second also, and the third, unto the seventh.

13 And last of all the woman died also.

14 Therefore in the resurrection whose wife shall she be of the seven? for they all had her.

15 Jesus answered and said unto them, Ye do err, not knowing the scriptures, nor the power of God.

16 For in the resurrection they neither marry, nor are given in marriage, but are as the angels of God in heaven.

17 But as touching the resurrection of the dead, have ye not read that which was spoken unto you by God, saying,

18 I am the God of Abraham, and the God of Isaac and the God of Jacob? God is not the God of the dead, but of the living.

19 And when the multitude heard *this,* they were astonished at his doctrine.

LII.

The Two Commandments.

A ND one of the scribes came, and having heard them reasoning together, and perceiving that he had answered them well, asked him, Which is the first commandment of all?

2 And Jesus answered him, The first of all the commandments *is*, Hear, O Israel; The Lord our God is one Lord:

3 And thou shalt love the Lord thy God with all thy heart, and with all thy soul, and with all thy mind, and with all thy strength: this *is* the first commandment.

4 And the second *is* like, *namely* this, Thou shalt love thy neighbour as thyself. There is none other commandment greater than these.

5 On these two commandments hang all the law and the prophets.

6 And the scribe said unto him, Well, Master, thou hast said the truth: for there is one God; and there is none other but he:

7 And to love him with all the heart, and with all the understanding, and with all the soul, and with all the strength, and to love *his* neighbour as himself, is more than all whole burnt offerings and sacrifices.

LIII.

Precepts, Pride, Hypocrisy, Swearing.

THEN spake Jesus to the multitude, and to his disciples,

2 Saying, The scribes and the Pharisees sit in Moses' seat:

3 All therefore whatsoever they bid you observe, *that* observe and do; but do not ye after their works: for they say, and do not.

4 For they bind heavy burdens and grievous to be borne, and lay *them* on men's shoulders; but they *themselves* will not move them with one of their fingers.

5 But all their works they do for to be seen of men: they make broad their phylacteries, and enlarge the borders of their garments,

6 And love the uppermost rooms at feasts, and the chief seats in the synagogues,

7 And greetings in the markets, and to be called of men, Rabbi, Rabbi.

8 But be not ye called Rabbi: for one is your Master, *even* Christ; and all ye are brethren.

9

9   And call no *man* your father upon the earth; for one is your Father, which is in heaven.

10   Neither be ye called masters: for one is your Master, *even* Christ.

11   But he that is greatest among you shall be your servant.

12   And whosoever shall exalt himself shall be abased; and he that shall humble himself shall be exalted.

13   ¶ But woe unto you, scribes and Pharisees, hypocrites! for ye shut up the kingdom of heaven against men: for ye neither go in *yourselves,* neither suffer ye them that are entering to go in.

14   Woe unto you, scribes and Pharisees, hypocrites! for ye devour widows' houses, and for a pretence make long prayer: therefore ye shall receive the greater damnation.

15   Woe unto you, scribes and Pharisees, hypocrites! for ye compass sea and land to make one proselyte, and when he is made, ye make him twofold more the child of hell than yourselves.

16   Woe unto you, *ye* blind guides, which say, Whosoever shall swear by the temple, it is nothing;

but whosoever shall swear by the gold of the temple, he is a debtor!

17   *Ye* fools and blind: for whether is greater, the gold, or the temple that sanctifieth the gold?

18   And, Whosoever shall swear by the altar, it is nothing; but whosoever sweareth by the gift that is upon it, he is guilty.

19   *Ye* fools and blind: for whether *is* greater, the gift, or the altar that sanctifieth the gift?

20   Whoso therefore shall swear by the altar, sweareth by it, and by all things thereon.

21   And whoso shall swear by the temple, sweareth by it, and by him that dwelleth therein.

22   And he that shall swear by heaven, sweareth by the throne of God, and by him that sitteth thereon.

23   Woe unto you, scribes and Pharisees, hypocrites! for ye pay tithe of mint and anise and cummin, and have omitted the weightier *matters* of the law, judgment, mercy, and faith: these ought ye to have done, and not to leave the other undone.

24   *Ye* blind guides, which strain at a gnat, and swallow a camel.

25 Woe unto you, scribes and Pharisees, hypocrites! for ye make clean the outside of the cup and of the platter, but within they are full of extortion and excess.

26 *Thou* blind Pharisee, cleanse first that *which is* within the cup and platter, that the outside of them may be clean also.

27 Woe unto you, scribes and Pharisees, hypocrites! for ye are like unto whited sepulchres, which indeed appear beautiful outward, but are within full of dead *men's* bones, and of all uncleanness.

28 Even so ye also outwardly appear righteous unto men, but within ye are full of hypocrisy and iniquity.

29 Woe unto you, scribes and Pharisees, hypocrites! because ye build the tombs of the prophets, and garnish the sepulchres of the righteous,

30 And say, If we had been in the days of our fathers, we would not have been partakers with them in the blood of the prophets.

31 Wherefore ye be witnesses unto yourselves, that ye are the children of them which killed the prophets.

32 Fill ye up then the measure of your fathers.

33 *Ye* serpents, *ye* generation of vipers, how can ye escape the damnation of hell?

LIV.

The Widow's Mite.

A ND Jesus sat over against the treasury, and beheld how the people cast money into the treasury: and many that were rich cast in much.

2 And there came a certain poor widow, and she threw in two mites, which make a farthing.

3 And he called *unto him* his disciples, and saith unto them, Verily I say unto you, That this poor widow hath cast more in, than all they which have cast into the treasury:

4 For all *they* did cast in of their abundance; but she of her want did cast in all that she had, *even* all her living.

LV.

Jerusalem and the Day of Judgment.

A ND Jesus went out, and departed from the temple: and his disciples came to *him* for to shew him the buildings of the temple.

2 And Jesus said unto them, See ye not all these things? verily I say unto you, There shall not be left here one stone upon another, that shall not be thrown down.

3 Then let them which be in Judea flee into the mountains:

4 Let him which is on the housetop not come down to take any thing out of his house:

5 Neither let him which is in the field return back to take his clothes.

6 And woe unto them that are with child, and to them that give suck in those days!

7 But pray ye that your flight be not in the winter, neither on the sabbath day:

8 For then shall be great tribulation, such as was not since the beginning of the world to this time, no, nor ever shall be.

9 ¶ Now learn a parable of the fig tree; When his branch is yet tender, and putteth forth leaves, ye know that summer *is* nigh:

10 So likewise ye, when ye shall see all these things, know that it is near *even* at the doors.

11 ¶ But of that day and hour knoweth no *man*, no, not the angels of heaven, but my Father only.

12 But as the days of Noe *were,* so shall also the coming of the Son of man be.

13 For as in the days that were before the flood they were eating and drinking, marrying and giving in marriage until the day that Noe entered into the ark,

14 And knew not until the flood came, and took them all away; so shall also the coming of the Son of man be.

15 Then shall two be in the field; the one shall be taken, and the other left.

16 Two *women shall be* grinding at the mill; the one shall be taken, and the other left.

17 Watch therefore: for ye know not what hour your Lord doth come.

18 But know this, that if the goodman of the house had known in what watch the thief would come, he would have watched, and would not have suffered his house to be broken up.

19 Therefore be ye also ready: for in such an hour as ye think not the Son of man cometh.

LVI.

The Faithful and Wise Servant.

WHO then is a faithful and wise servant, whom his lord hath made ruler over his household, to give them meat in due season?

2   Blessed *is* that servant, whom his lord when he cometh shall find so doing.

3   Verily I say unto you, That he shall make him ruler over all his goods.

4   But and if that evil servant shall say in his heart, My lord delayeth his coming;

5   And shall begin to smite *his* fellow-servants, and to eat and drink with the drunken;

6   The lord of that servant shall come in a day when he looketh not for *him*, and in an hour that he is not aware of,

7   And shall cut him asunder, and appoint *him* his portion with the hypocrites: there shall be weeping and gnashing of teeth.

LVII.

Parable of the Ten Virgins.

THEN shall the kingdom of heaven be likened unto ten virgins, which took their lamps, and went forth to meet the bridegroom.

2 And five of them were wise, and five *were* foolish.

3 They that *were* foolish took their lamps, and took no oil with them:

4 But the wise took oil in their vessels with their lamps.

5 While the bridegroom tarried, they all slumbered and slept.

6 And at midnight there was a cry made, Behold, the bridegroom cometh; go ye out to meet him.

7 Then all those virgins arose, and trimmed their lamps.

8 And the foolish said unto the wise, Give us of your oil; for our lamps are gone out.

9 But the wise answered, saying, *Not so;* lest there be not enough for us and you: but go ye rather to them that sell, and buy for yourselves.

10   And while they went to buy, the bridegroom came; and they that were ready went in with him to the marriage: and the door was shut.

11   Afterward came also the other virgins, saying, Lord, Lord, open to us.

12   But he answered and said, Verily I say unto you, I know you not.

13   Watch, therefore, for ye know neither the day nor the hour wherein the Son of man cometh.

LVIII.

Parable of the Talents.

FOR *the kingdom of heaven is* as a man travelling into a far country, *who* called his own servants, and delivered unto them his goods.

2   And unto one he gave five talents, to another two, and to another one; to every man according to his several ability; and straightway took his journey.

3   Then he that had received the five talents went and traded with the same, and made *them* other five talents.

4　And likewise he that *had received* two, he also gained other two.

5　But he that had received one went and digged in the earth, and hid his lord's money.

6　After a long time the lord of those servants cometh, and reckoneth with them.

7　And so he that had received five talents came and brought other five talents, saying, Lord, thou deliveredst unto me five talents: behold, I have gained beside them five talents more.

8　His lord said unto him, Well done, *thou* good and faithful servant: thou hast been faithful over a few things, I will make thee ruler over many things: enter thou into the joy of thy lord.

9　He also that had received two talents came and said, Lord, thou deliveredst unto me two talents: behold, I have gained two other talents beside them.

10　His lord said unto him, Well done, good and faithful servant; thou hast been faithful over a few things, I will make thee ruler over many things; enter thou into the joy of thy lord.

11　Then he which had received the one talent came and said, Lord, I knew thee that thou art an hard man, reaping where thou hast not sown, and gathering where thou hast not strawed:

12 And I was afraid, and went and hid thy talent in the earth: lo, *there* thou hast *that is* thine.

13 His lord answered and said unto him, *Thou* wicked and slothful servant, thou knewest that I reap where I sowed not, and gather where I have not strawed:

14 Thou oughtest therefore to have put my money to the exchangers, and *then* at my coming I should have received mine own with usury.

15 Take therefore the talent from him, and give *it* unto him which hath ten talents.

16 For unto every one that hath shall be given, and he shall have abundance: but from him that hath not shall be taken away even that which he hath.

17 And cast ye the unprofitable servant into outer darkness: there shall be weeping and gnash-ing of teeth.

LIX.

The Day of Judgment.

AND take heed to yourselves, lest at any time your hearts be overcharged with surfeiting, and drunkenness, and cares of this life, and *so* that day come upon you unawares.

2 For as a snare shall it come on all them that dwell on the face of the whole earth.

3 Watch ye therefore, and pray always, that ye may be accounted worthy to escape all these things that shall come to pass, and to stand before the Son of man.

4 When the Son of man shall come in his glory, and all the holy angels with him, then shall he sit upon the throne of his glory:

5 And before him shall be gathered all nations: and he shall separate them one from another, as a shepherd divideth *his* sheep from the goats:

6 And he shall set the sheep on his right hand, but the goats on the left.

7 Then shall the King say unto them on his right hand, Come, ye blessed of my Father, inherit

the kingdom prepared for you from the foundation of the world:

8   For I was an hungred, and ye gave me meat: I was thirsty, and ye gave me drink: I was a stranger, and ye took me in:

9   Naked, and ye clothed me: I was sick, and ye visited me: I was in prison, and ye came unto me.

10   Then shall the righteous answer him, saying, Lord, when saw we thee an hungred, and fed *thee?* or thirsty, and gave *thee* drink?

11   When saw we thee a stranger, and took *thee* in? or naked, and clothed *thee?*

12   Or when saw we thee sick, or in prison, and came unto thee?

13   And the King shall answer and say unto them, Verily I say unto you, Inasmuch as ye have done *it* unto one of the least of these my brethren, ye have done *it* unto me.

14   Then shall he say also unto them on the left hand, Depart from me, ye cursed, into everlasting fire, prepared for the devil and his angels:

15   For I was an hungred, and ye gave me no meat: I was thirsty, and ye gave me no drink:

16 I was a stranger, and ye took me not in: naked, and ye clothed me not: sick, and in prison, and ye visited me not.

17 Then shall they also answer him, saying, Lord, when saw we thee an hungred, or athirst, or a stranger, or naked, or sick, or in prison, and did not minister unto thee?

18 Then shall he answer them, saying, Verily, I say unto you, Inasmuch as ye did *it* not to one of the least of these, ye did *it* not to me.

19 And these shall go away into everlasting punishment: but the righteous into life eternal.

LX.

A Woman Anointeth Him.

AFTER two days was *the feast of* the passover, and of unleavened bread: and the chief priests and the scribes sought how they might take him by craft, and put *him* to death.

2 But they said, Not on the feast *day*, lest there be an uproar of the people.

3 ¶ And being in Bethany in the house of Simon the leper, as he sat at meat, there came a

woman having an alabaster box of ointment of spikenard very precious; and she brake the box, and poured *it* on his head.

4 And there were some that had indignation within themselves, and said, Why was this waste of the ointment made?

5 For it might have been sold for more than three hundred pence, and have been given to the poor. And they murmured against her.

6 And Jesus said, Let her alone; why trouble ye her? she hath wrought a good work on me.

7 For ye have the poor with you always, and whensoever ye will ye may do them good: but me ye have not always.

8 She hath done what she could: she is come aforehand to anoint my body to the burying.

LXI.

Judas Undertakes to Point Out Jesus.

THEN one of the twelve, called Judas Iscariot, went unto the chief priests,

2 And said *unto them*, What will ye give me, and I will deliver him unto you? And they covenanted with him for thirty pieces of silver.

3 And from that time he sought opportunity to betray him.

LXII.

Precepts to His Disciples, Washes their Feet. Trouble of Mind and Prayer.

NOW the first *day* of the *feast of* unleavened bread the disciples came to Jesus, saying unto him, Where wilt thou that we prepare for thee to eat the passover?

2 And he said, Go into the city to such a man, and say unto him, The Master saith, My time is at hand; I will keep the passover at thy house with my disciples.

3 And the disciples did as Jesus had appointed them; and they made ready the passover.

4 Now when the even was come, he sat down with the twelve.

5 And there was also a strife among them, which of them should be accounted the greatest.

6 And he said unto them, The kings of the Gentiles exercised lordship over them; and they that

10

exercise authority upon them are called benefactors.

7   But ye *shall* not *be* so: but he that is greatest among you, let him be as the younger; and he that is chief, as he that doth serve.

8   For whether *is* greater, he that sitteth at meat, or he that serveth? *is* not he that sitteth at meat? but I am among you as he that serveth.

9   And supper being ended, the devil having now put into the heart of Judas Iscariot, Simon's *son*, to betray him;

10   He riseth from supper, and laid aside his garments; and took a towel, and girded himself.

11   After that he poureth water into a bason, and began to wash the disciples' feet, and to wipe *them* with the towel wherewith he was girded.

12   Then cometh he to Simon Peter; and Peter saith unto him, Lord, dost thou wash my feet?

13   Jesus answered and said unto him, What I do thou knowest not now; but thou shalt know hereafter.

14   Peter saith unto him, Thou shalt never wash my feet.   Jesus answered him, If I wash thee not, thou hast no part with me.

15 Simon Peter saith unto him, Lord, not my feet only, but also *my* hands and *my* head.

16 Jesus saith to Him, He that is washed needeth not save to wash *his* feet, but is clean every whit: and ye are clean, but not all.

17 For he knew who should betray him; therefore said he, Ye are not all clean.

18 So after he had washed their feet, and had taken his garments, and was set down again, he said unto them, Know ye what I have done to you?

19 Ye call me Master and Lord: and ye say well; for *so* I am.

20 If I then, *your* Lord and Master, have washed your feet; ye also ought to wash one another's feet.

21 For I have given you an example, that ye should do as I have done to you.

22 Verily, verily, I say unto you, The servant is not greater than his lord; neither he that is sent greater than he that sent him.

23 If ye know these things, happy are ye if ye do them.

24 When Jesus had thus said, he was troubled in spirit, and testified, and said, Verily, verily, I say unto you, that one of you shall betray me.

25 Then the disciples looked one on another, doubting of whom he spake.

26 Now there was leaning on Jesus' bosom one of his disciples whom Jesus loved.

27 Simon Peter therefore beckoned to him, that he should ask who it should be of whom he spake.

28 He then lying on Jesus' breast saith unto him, Lord, who is it?

29 Jesus answered, He it is, to whom I shall give a sop, when I have dipped *it*. And when he had dipped the sop, he gave *it* to Judas Iscariot, *the son* of Simon.

30 ¶ Therefore, when he was gone out, Jesus said, Now is the Son of man glorified, and God is glorified in him.

31 A new commandment I give unto you, That ye love one another; as I have loved you, that ye also love one another.

32 By this shall all *men* know that ye are my disciples, if ye have love one to another.

33 Then said Jesus unto them, All ye shall be offended because of me this night: for it is writ-

ten, I will smite the shepherd, and the sheep of the flock shall be scattered abroad.

34 Peter answered and said unto him, Though all *men* shall be offended because of thee, *yet* will I never be offended.

35 And he said unto him, Lord, I am ready to go with thee, both into prison, and to death.

36 And he said, I tell thee, Peter, the cock shall not crow this day, before that thou shalt thrice deny that thou knowest me.

37 Peter said unto him, Though I should die with thee, yet will I not deny thee. Likewise also said all the disciples.

38 ¶ Then cometh Jesus with them unto a place called Gethsemane, and said unto the disciples, Sit ye here, while I go and pray yonder.

39 And he took with him Peter and the two sons of Zebedee, and began to be sorrowful and very heavy.

40 Then saith he unto them, My soul is exceeding sorrowful, even unto death: tarry ye here, and watch with me.

41 And he went a little farther, and fell on his face, and prayed, saying, O my Father, if it be pos-

sible, let this cup pass from me: nevertheless not as I will, but as thou *wilt*.

42   And he cometh unto the disciples, and findeth them asleep, and saith unto Peter, What, could ye not watch with me one hour?

43   Watch and pray, that ye enter not into temptation: the spirit indeed *is* willing, but the flesh *is* weak.

44   He went away again the second time, and prayed, saying, O my Father, if this cup may not pass away from me, except I drink it, thy will be done.

45   And he came and found them asleep again: for their eyes were heavy.

46   And he left them, and went away again, and prayed the third time, saying the same words.

47   Then cometh he to his disciples, and saith unto them, Sleep on now, and take *your* rest: behold, the hour is at hand, and the Son of man is betrayed into the hands of sinners.

LXIII.

Judas Conducts the Officers to Jesus.

WHEN Jesus had spoken these words, he went forth with his disciples over the brook Cedron, where was a garden, into the which he entered, and his disciples.

2 And Judas also, which betrayed him, knew the place: for Jesus ofttimes resorted thither with his disciples.

3 Judas then, having received a band of *men* and officers from the chief priests and Pharisees, cometh thither with lanterns and torches and weapons.

4 Now he that betrayed him gave them a sign, saying, Whomsoever I shall kiss, that same is he: hold him fast.

5 And forthwith he came to Jesus, and said, Hail, master; and kissed him.

6 And Jesus said unto him, Friend, wherefore art thou come? Then came they, and laid hands on Jesus, and took him.

LXIV.

He is Arrested and Carried Before Caiaphas, the High Priest and is Condemned.

JESUS therefore, knowing all things that should come upon him, went forth, and said unto them, Whom seek ye?

2 They answered him, Jesus of Nazareth. Jesus saith unto them, I am *he.* And Judas also, which betrayed him, stood with them.

3 As soon then as he had said unto them, I am *he,* they went backward, and fell to the ground.

4 Then asked he them again, Whom seek ye? And they said, Jesus of Nazareth.

5 Jesus answered, I have told you that I am *he;* if therefore ye seek me, let these go their way:

6 And Jesus said unto him, Friend, wherefore art thou come? Then came they, and laid hands on Jesus, and took him.

7 And, behold, one of them which were with Jesus stretched out *his* hand, and drew his sword, and struck a servant of the high priest's, and smote off his ear.

8 Then said Jesus unto him, Put up again thy sword into his place: for all they that take the sword shall perish with the sword.

9 In that same hour said Jesus to the multitudes, Are ye come out as against a thief with swords and staves for to take me? I sat daily with you teaching in the temple, and ye laid no hold on me.

10 But all this was done, that the scriptures of the prophets might be fulfilled. Then all the disciples forsook him, and fled.

11 And there followed him a certain young man, having a linen cloth cast about *his* naked *body;* and the young men laid hold on him:

12 And he left the linen cloth, and fled from them naked.

13 ¶ And they that had laid hold on Jesus led *him* away to Caiaphas the high priest, where the scribes and the elders were assembled.

14 And Simon Peter followed Jesus, and *so did* another disciple: that disciple was known unto the high priest, and went in with Jesus into the palace of the high priest.

15   But Peter stood at the door without.   Then went out that other disciple, which was known unto the high priest, and spake unto her that kept the door, and brought in Peter.

16   Then saith the damsel that kept the door, unto Peter, Art not thou also *one* of this man's disciples?   He saith, I am not.

17   And the servants and officers stood there, who had made a fire of coals; for it was cold: and they warmed themselves: and Peter stood with them, and warmed himself.

18   ¶ And Simon Peter stood and warmed himself.   They said therefore unto him, Art not thou also *one* of his disciples?   He denied *it,* and said, I am not.

19   One of the servants of the high priest, being *his* kinsman whose ear Peter cut off, saith, Did not I see thee in the garden with him?

20   Peter then denied again: and immediately the cock crew.

21   And Peter remembered the word of Jesus, which said unto him, Before the cock crow, thou shalt deny me thrice.   And he went out, and wept bitterly.

22 ¶ The high priest then asked Jesus of his disciples, and of his doctrine.

23 Jesus answered him, I spake openly to the world; I ever taught in the synagogue, and in the temple, whither the Jews always resort; and in secret have I said nothing.

24 Why askest thou me? ask them which heard me, what I have said unto them: behold, they know what I said.

25 And when he had thus spoken, one of the officers which stood by struck Jesus with the palm of his hand, saying, Answerest thou the high priest so?

26 Jesus answered him, If I have spoken evil, bear witness of the evil; but if well, why smitest thou me?

27 And the chief priests and all the council sought for witness against Jesus to put him to death; and found none.

28 For many bare false witness against him, but their witness agreed not together.

29 And there arose certain, and bare false witness against him, saying,

30 We heard him say, I will destroy this temple that is made with hands, and within three days I will build another made without hands.

31   But neither so did their witness agree together.

32   And the high priest stood up in the midst, and asked Jesus, saying, Answerest thou nothing? what *is it which* these witness against thee?

33   But he held his peace, and answered nothing. Again the high priest asked him, and said unto him, Art thou the Christ, the Son of the Blessed?

34   Art thou the Christ? tell us. _And he said unto them, If I tell you, ye will not believe:

35   And if I also ask *you,* ye will not answer me, nor let *me* go.

36   Then said they all, Art thou then the Son of God?   And he said unto them, Ye say that I am.

37   Then the high priest rent his clothes, and saith, What need we any further witnesses?

38   Ye have heard the blasphemy: what think ye? And they all condemned him to be guilty of death.

39   And some began to spit on him, and to cover his face, and to buffet him, and to say unto him, Prophesy: and the servants did strike him with the palms of their hands.

OF JESUS OF NAZARETH.

LXV.

Is then Carried to Pilate.

THEN led they Jesus from Caiaphas unto the hall of judgment: and it was early; and they themselves went not into the judgment hall, lest they should be defiled; but that they might eat the passover.

2 Pilate then went out unto them, and said, What accusation bring ye against this man?

3 They answered and said unto him, If he were not a malefactor, we would not have delivered him up unto thee.

4 Then said Pilate unto them, Take ye him, and judge him according to your law. The Jews therefore said unto him, It is not lawful for us to put any man to death.

5 Then Pilate entered into the judgment hall again, and called Jesus, and said unto him, Art thou the King of the Jews?

6 Jesus answered him, Sayest thou this thing of thyself, or did others tell it thee of me?

7   Pilate answered, Am I a Jew?   Thine own nation and the chief priests have delivered thee unto me: what hast thou done?

8   Jesus answered, My kingdom is not of this world; if my kingdom were of this world, then would my servants fight, that I should not be delivered to the Jews: but now is my kingdom not from hence.

9   Pilate therefore said unto him, Art thou a king then?   Jesus answered, Thou sayest that I am a king.   To this end was I born, and for this cause came I into the world, that I should bear witness unto the truth.   Every one that is of the truth heareth my voice.

10   Pilate saith unto him, What is truth?   And when he had said this, he went out again unto the Jews, and saith unto them, I find in him no fault *at all*.

11   And they were the more fierce, saying, He stirreth up the people, teaching throughout all Jewry, beginning from Galilee to this place.

12   Then said Pilate unto him, Hearest thou not how many things they witness against thee?

LXVI.

Who Sends Him to Herod.

WHEN Pilate heard of Galilee, he asked whether the man were a Galilean.

2 And as soon as he knew that he belonged unto Herod's jurisdiction, he sent him to Herod, who himself also was at Jerusalem at that time.

3 ¶ And when Herod saw Jesus, he was exceeding glad: for he was desirous to see him of a long *season,* because he had heard many things of him; and he hoped to have seen some miracle done by him.

4 Then he questioned with him in many words; but he answered him nothing.

5 And the chief priests and scribes stood and vehemently accused him.

6 And Herod with his men of war set him at naught, and mocked *him,* and arrayed him in a gorgeous robe, and sent him again to Pilate.

7 And the same day Pilate and Herod were made friends together: for before they were at enmity between themselves.

THE LIFE AND MORALS

LXVII.

Receives Him Back, Scourges and Delivers Him to Execution.

A ND Pilate, when he had called together the chief priests and the rulers and the people,

2 Said unto them, Ye have brought this man unto me, as one that perverteth the people: and, behold, I, having examined *him* before you, have found no fault in this man touching those things whereof ye accuse him:

3 No, nor yet Herod: for I sent you to him; and, lo, nothing worthy of death is done unto him.

4 I will therefore chastise him, and release *him*.

5 ¶ Now at *that* feast the governor was wont to release unto the people a prisoner, whom they would.

6 And they had then a notable prisoner, called Barabbas.

7 Therefore when they were gathered together, Pilate said unto them, Whom will ye that I release unto you? Barabbas, or Jesus which is called Christ?

8 For he knew that for envy they had delivered him.

9 ¶ When he was set down on the judgment seat, his wife sent unto him, saying, Have thou nothing to do with that just man: for I have suffered many things this day in a dream because of him.

10 But the chief priests and elders persuaded the multitude that they should ask Barabbas, and destroy Jesus.

11 The governor answered and said unto them, Whether of the twain will ye that I release unto you? They said, Barabbas.

12 Pilate saith unto them, What shall I do then with Jesus which is called Christ? *They* all say unto him, Let him be crucified.

13 And the governor said, Why, what evil hath he done? But they cried out the more, saying, Let him be crucified.

14 Then released he Barabbas unto them: and when he had scourged Jesus, he delivered *him* to be crucified.

11

THE LIFE AND MORALS

LXVIII.

His Crucifixion, Death, and Burial.

THEN the soldiers of the governor took Jesus into the common hall, and gathered unto him the whole band of *soldiers.*

2 And when they had platted a crown of thorns, they put *it* upon his head, and a reed in his right hand: and they bowed the knee before him, and mocked him, saying, Hail, King of the Jews!

3 And they spit upon him, and took the reed and smote him on the head.

4 And after that they had mocked him, they took the robe off from him, and put his own raiment on him, and led him away to crucify *him.*

5 ¶ Then Judas, which had betrayed him, when he saw that he was condemned, repented himself, and brought again the thirty pieces of silver to the chief priests and elders,

6 Saying, I have sinned in that I have betrayed the innocent blood. And they said, What *is that* to us? see thou *to that.*

7 And he cast down the pieces of silver in the temple, and departed, and went and hanged himself.

8 And the chief priests took the silver pieces, and said, It is not lawful for to put them into the treasury, because it is the price of blood.

9 And they took counsel, and bought with them the potter's field, to bury strangers in.

10 Wherefore that field was called, The field of blood, unto this day.

11 ¶ And as they led him away, they laid hold upon one Simon, a Cyrenian, coming out of the country, and on him they laid the cross, that he might bear *it* after Jesus.

12 And there followed him a great company of people, and of women, which also bewailed and lamented him.

13 But Jesus turning unto them said, Daughters of Jerusalem, weep not for me, but weep for yourselves, and for your children.

14 For, behold, the days are coming, in the which they shall say, Blessed *are* the barren, and the wombs that never bare, and the paps which never gave suck.

15 Then shall they begin to say to the mountains, Fall on us; and to the hills, Cover us.

16 For if they do these things in a green tree, what shall be done in the dry?

17 ¶ And there were also two other, malefactors, led with him to be put to death.

18 And he bearing his cross went forth into a place called *the place* of a skull, which is called in the Hebrew, Golgotha:

19 Where they crucified him, and two other with him, on either side one, and Jesus in the midst.

20 ¶ And Pilate wrote a title, and put *it* on the cross. And the writing was, JESUS OF NAZARETH THE KING OF THE JEWS.

21 This title then read many of the Jews: for the place where Jesus was crucified was nigh to the city: and it was written in Hebrew, *and* Greek, *and* Latin.

22 Then said the chief priests of the Jews to Pilate, Write not, The King of the Jews; but that he said, I am King of the Jews.

23 Pilate answered, What I have written I have written.

24 ¶ Then the soldiers, when they had crucified Jesus, took his garments, and made four parts, to every soldier a part; and also *his* coat: now the coat was without seam, woven from the top throughout.

25 They said therefore among themselves, Let us not rend it, but cast lots for it, whose it shall be: that the scripture might be fulfilled, which saith, They parted my raiment among them, and for my vesture they did cast lots. These things therefore the soldiers did.

26 ¶ And they that passed by reviled him, wagging their heads,

27 And saying, Thou that destroyest the temple, and buildest *it* in three days, save thyself. If thou be the Son of God, come down from the cross.

28 Likewise also the chief priests mocking *him*, with the scribes and elders, said,

29 He saved others; himself he cannot save. If he be the King of Israel, let him now come down from the cross, and we will believe him.

30 He trusted in God; let him deliver him now, if he will have him: for he said, I am the Son of God.

31 ¶ And one of the malefactors which were hanged railed on him, saying, If thou be Christ, save thyself and us.

32 But the other answering rebuked him, saying, Dost not thou fear God, seeing thou art in the same condemnation?

33 And we indeed justly; for we receive the due reward of our deeds: but this man hath done nothing amiss.

34 Then said Jesus, Father, forgive them; for they know not what they do. And they parted his raiment, and cast lots.

35 ¶ Now there stood by the cross of Jesus his mother, and his mother's sister, Mary the *wife* of Cleophas, and Mary Magdalene.

36 When Jesus therefore saw his mother, and the disciple standing by, whom he loved, he saith unto his mother, Woman, behold thy son!

37 Then saith he to the disciple, Behold thy mother! And from that hour that disciple took her unto his own *home*.

38 And about the ninth hour Jesus cried with a loud voice, saying, Eli, Eli, lama sabachthani? that is to say, My God, my God, why hast thou forsaken me?

39 Some of them that stood there, when they heard *that*, said, This *man* calleth for Elias.

40 And straightway one of them ran, and took a spunge, and filled *it* with vinegar, and put *it* on a reed, and gave him to drink.

41 The rest said, Let be, let us see whether Elias will come to save him.

42 ¶ Jesus, when he had cried again with a loud voice, yielded up the ghost.

43 And many women were there beholding afar off, which followed Jesus from Galilee, ministering unto him:

44 Among which was Mary Magdalene, and Mary the mother of James and Joses, and the mother of Zebedee's children.

LXIX.

His Burial.

THE Jews therefore, because it was the preparation, that the bodies should not remain upon the cross on the sabbath day, (for that sabbath day was an high day,) besought Pilate that their legs might be broken, and *that* they might be taken away.

2 Then came the soldiers, and brake the legs of the first, and of the other which was crucified with him.

3 But when they came to Jesus, and saw that he was dead already, they brake not his legs:

4 But one of the soldiers with a spear pierced his side, and forthwith came there out blood and water.

5 ¶ And after this Joseph of Arimathaea, being a disciple of Jesus, but secretly for fear of the Jews, besought Pilate that he might take away the body of Jesus: and Pilate gave *him* leave. He came therefore, and took the body of Jesus.

6 And there came also Nicodemus, which at the first came to Jesus by night, and brought a mixture of myrrh and aloes, about an hundred pound *weight*.

7 Then took they the body of Jesus, and wound it in linen clothes with the spices, as the manner of the Jews is to bury.

8 Now in the place where he was crucified there was a garden; and in the garden a new sepulchre, wherein never man yet laid.

9 There laid they Jesus: and rolled a great stone to the door of the sepulchre, and departed.